Plugged In
and Turned On

Plugged In and Turned On

Planning, Coordinating,
and Managing
Computer-Supported
Instruction

Charles H. McCain

CORWIN PRESS, INC.
A Sage Publications Company
Thousand Oaks, California

For information address:

Corwin Press, Inc.
A Sage Publications Company
2455 Teller Road
Thousand Oaks, California 91320
E-mail: order@corwin.sagepub.com

SAGE Publications Ltd.
6 Bonhill Street
London EC2A 4PU
United Kingdom

SAGE Publications India Pvt. Ltd.
M-32 Market
Greater Kailash I
New Delhi 110 048 India

Printed in the United States of America

Library of Congress Cataloging-in-Publication Data

McCain, Charles H.
   Plugged in and turned on : planning, coordinating, and managing
computer-supported instruction / Charles H. McCain.
      p. cm.
   Includes bibliographical references (p.) and index.
   ISBN 0-8039-6431-5 (cloth : acid-free paper). — ISBN
0-8039-6432-3 (pbk.: acid-free paper)
      1. School buildings—Data processing. 2. School facilities—Data
processing. 3. Computer-assisted instruction—Planning.
4. Computer managed instruction—Planning. I. Title.
LB3209.M36 1996
371.6'21'0285—dc20   96-4528
                                                                              CIP

This book is printed on acid-free paper.

96 97 98 99 10 9 8 7 6 5 4 3 2 1

Sage Production Editor: Michèle Lingre

Contents

Foreword

My own experience, garnered from more than 20 years as chief information officer in the nation's largest corporations, is that the success of computer technology is rarely attributable to the technology per se. Almost always the management process is the determining factor. As a long-time board member of the Westchester County Education Coalition, I have observed this rule to be as applicable in schools as it is in industry. During my children's lifetimes, I've seen computing move from a technical specialty to a ubiquitous tool for everyone. Schools now struggle to come to grips with the financial and pedagogical implications of this rapid and dramatic change.

Educators may be aware of technology, but typically they have been blind to the need for the supporting infrastructure and management processes. Mostly, this is because the print and TV media focus on the glitz, and, even if the media are aware of it, they pay scant attention to what goes on behind the scenes. Computer companies create a din of computer hype, and educators get little support for the necessary infrastructure.

This book neither mentions products nor dwells on the details of any technology. Rather, it is a how-to-succeed book for educators concerned about the introduction of technology, and it deals with all the things the computer salesperson never told you. It is also about the practical aspects of a management philosophy attuned to computer technology in schools.

Plugged In and Turned On has a unique perspective, and it should be required reading for school board members, principals, school technical specialists, and educators at the state level.

Raymond S. Perry
Clinical Professor, Computer and Information Systems
Graduate School of Business Administration
University of Michigan

Preface

Few schools are prepared for the momentous consequences of the computer revolution. It is the most significant change in knowledge technology since the late 15th century, when Johannes Gutenberg invented printing with movable type. Computers and telecommunications have redefined how knowledge is stored, transmitted, presented, and even created.

In the 1980s, the U.S. professional and clerical workforce shifted from using pad and pencil to using desktop computers. As a direct consequence, the workplace largely had to be reconstructed. The buildings had to be renovated, operating procedures and policies had to be rewritten, and the jobs themselves had to be reinvented. Often, because companies did not understand what was happening until the technical shift was already a ground swell, the changes were made reactively. Those companies are now saddled with a suboptimum, expensive patchwork of fixes—fixes that are proving difficult or virtually impossible to remedy.

I believe it is safe to assume that there will be a computer on every desk in many, if not most, classrooms within the next decade. In the transition, schools will have thrust on them the same infrastructure issues as did industry. Drawing on the experience of 35 years in developing and managing computer technology, I am writing to alert educators at the state and local levels to the host of changes that must be made. Schools that seize this window of opportunity to manage the transition actively will realize the full benefits of their human and capital investment. As in industry, those who fail to do so will spend more, and they will have far less success.

This jargon-free book addresses the fundamental overhaul of the educational infrastructure that is necessary for classroom technology to function: Management practices, buildings, classrooms and furniture, staffing, teacher support, and a wide range of policies all must change. It is structured to be read on three levels.

- The summary level consists of the introduction to the book and a synopsis preceding each chapter. In less than an hour, a reader can grasp the central ideas.
- The intermediate level is the main text. It thoroughly addresses all the issues and a range of possible solutions. No special knowledge is needed to follow the discussion.
- The third, the most technical level, is developed in extensive appendices that provide detailed, practical guidelines for those responsible for managing technical programs. Also, endnotes and a comprehensive reference section facilitate further research.

I hope that with this insight, the unfortunate experiences of many corporations can be avoided by educators and the full potential of the opportunities realized.

Acknowledgments

Writing a book such as this is a humbling experience. I have come to realize that I am less the creator than I am the scribe for countless associates who, by example and admonition, have helped me understand what it takes to make the information revolution succeed. I also have been particularly fortunate to have friends in industry, research, and education whose candid criticisms have been invaluable. Frederick Dyer, William Elberty, Karen Loop, Raymond Perry, and Jacob Waller each contributed unique perspectives. As to putting the words on paper, Marcia Bonner has greatly improved the readability of the book without substantive damage to my ego; as a grammarian and author, her suggestions have made this book suitable for human consumption. And through it all my wife, Ardis, has provided me with encouragement, forbearance, and an unerring nose for pomposity and jargon.

Introduction

The information age is not approaching—it has arrived! It arrived not in the sense of having reached a final destination, but rather as a long journey well underway. The direction has been clearly established even though the more distant objectives are only faintly perceived. Significantly, it is both a journey that is unavoidable and one for which the educational establishment is prepared inadequately.

In 1995, between one third and one half of U.S. households had a computer (Yankelovich Partners, 1995)[1]; one study found that more than one third of the nation's students used a computer at home and three quarters of children often or sometimes used them for schoolwork (Times Mirror Center, 1994).

The inundation continues unabated. In 1995, desktop computer sales were $23 million; this was a 22% increase from 1994, and a high growth rate is anticipated to continue throughout 1996. In recent years, about one third of the sales have been for home use. These statistics, however, understate the flow of machines into homes, because some of the sales to businesses displace machines that eventually appear in homes. With home personal computer (PC) prices in the $1,500 to $2,000 range, it is not surprising that more high-income than low-income households have computers: More than half of the families with incomes of $50,000 and over have computers as compared to 11% for those with an income of less than $20,000 (Times Mirror Center, 1994). These statistics represent a dilemma for schools that must prepare graduates for an information-based economy in which computer literacy is becoming a job prerequisite. If many students use computers at home for schoolwork but others lack that opportunity, how does the school provide for the economically disadvantaged? The peril of developing a high-tech overclass and a low-tech underclass is obvious. Indeed, the National Commission for Employment Policy reports that high school graduates who used a computer in their work earned 17% more than those who did not (Rose, 1994).[2]

Forty years ago, the information age began with the use of computers in office buildings and factories. In the early 1980s, the PC revolution moved computing from the controlled environment of the data center to wherever the user happened to be—office, home, or vehicle. Concurrently, the role of the computer has grown from being employed only in the execution of rote, mundane tasks, such as customer billing, into being used as a multifaceted aid to all those who work with information.

The explosive growth of inexpensive computer technology in the workplace has been paralleled by two equally dramatic changes in telecommunications. Fiber-optic cables with digital signals are now expanding the transmission capacity of land lines by a factor of a thousand or more; also, wireless networks are extending communications into every imaginable place. Low-cost communications, coupled with inexpensive computers, already have revolutionized the workplace. Information work (handling information as opposed to materials or goods) now accounts for 70% or more of the labor hours in the United States (Strassmann, 1995), and 85% of office workers use a computer or terminal (Steelcase, Inc., 1991b). Thomas L. Whistler (1964) at the University of Chicago succinctly describes the future: "[We] are going to have to learn to be managers in a world where the organization will come close to consisting of all chiefs and one Indian. The Indian, of course, is the computer."

Our democracy and our economy depend on an educated populace, yet oddly, primary and secondary schools have been the last segments of the economy to move from a 19th-century industrial age into the information age. Only recently and in the most forward-looking schools, has computer technology begun to change the teaching process directly.

The forces acting to transform education are evident everywhere.

- Federal agencies are fostering information technology programs, such as the proposed "information highway," directed at bringing schools and the population at large into the information age. A Library of Congress program—the National Digital Library—already has commenced digitizing five million of the most popular items in its collection, which spans 500 miles of bookshelves and includes 14 million photographs.
- The telephone, television, film, publishing, and computer companies are jockeying to position themselves in the digital information market, which will encompass every workplace, home, and schoolroom.
- State education agencies are offering schools encouragement and funds for computers and software. In addition, school boards, parent groups, and even businesses are funding computer acquisitions for schools.
- Technology particularly suited to the education market is proliferating, and its cost is plummeting. Also, many teachers just entering the profession are already computer literate and urging change.

Computer and communications technologies will improve the quality of learning in the public school system dramatically in three ways:

- The learning process, which presently is based on the transference of knowledge by a teacher "teaching" the material, will shift toward a student-centered process with the teacher guiding the student's personal exploration of the subject material.
- The universe of available subject material will extend beyond the resources of the classroom; information sources, pre-

viously inaccessible, can materialize in a few keystrokes. The functions of both teacher and student will change, and both will find their new roles more rewarding.

• Affordable technology will engage the minds of many who would otherwise fail to be captured by the excitement of learning. The learning process becomes student driven rather than teacher driven and, therefore, more adaptable to children with differing learning styles and types of intelligence (Armstrong, 1994).[3] The success of U.S. public education can be measured by how well it has met the needs of the majority of students. It has failed in some respects, because it has not adequately addressed those children falling outside the conventional boundaries (U.S. Department of Education, 1994; Whalen, 1994).[4,5] Computer-based learning will help close that gap.

New technology can never overlay existing physical facilities and institutions successfully without having far-reaching consequences. Electric motors, automobiles, and television, for example, all have necessitated changes to our landscape, factories, homes, occupations, and laws. Each new technology has required a new supporting infrastructure to function effectively. Likewise, computer technology is occasioning far-reaching changes, and many of them will affect schools.

Few of today's school buildings are appropriate for the new technology. Their heating, ventilation, and air-conditioning (HVAC) systems are inadequate for the heat generated by the machines. Their electrical systems are undersized, and computer networks to link students to learning resources such as teachers and libraries are nonexistent. Worse, the construction of these buildings does not lend itself to easy rectification of these and other deficiencies.

Just as a new standard must evolve for the construction of school buildings and classrooms, new policies and practices must be formulated to carry out the day-to-day operations of these new technologies. Policies and procedures are as essential to the technology infrastructure as traffic laws and highway etiquette are to the automotive infrastructure.

To date, most school computers have been used to enhance the traditional instructional techniques; they are used for drill and practice as electronic workbooks and as word processors. The new technology gradually will bring about a new teaching paradigm. The teacher's role as lecturer will diminish in favor of a role as coach and facilitator. The existing model is one of the teacher as the primary giver of information, supported by textbooks and occasional audiovisual presentations. The new model for the teacher is one of directing and facilitating the learning process of individual students who each have almost instantaneous access to a wide variety of learning experiences and knowledge sources.

The transition to new teaching methods is hardly trivial. Most of the present teaching staff have had years of college training and classroom success with the current paradigm; they may have little enthusiasm for change. Moreover, lacking training and new exemplars, many are intimidated by the technology. It is essential to recognize the difficulty of the changes required. An infrastructure must be created to support teachers in their learning adventures. There must be formal training, informal coaching, and prompt technical support. There also must be easily replicated examples of classroom success and, above all, enthusiastic leadership.

Information technology can only flourish in conjunction with an adequate infrastructure of physical plant, practices, and people. This book explores those issues most essential to success. The concluding appendices are more concrete and prescriptive; they approach many of these issues in terms of off-the-shelf models adaptable to any school system.

This book, however, does not touch on the crucial issue of teaching methods; the necessary changes in teaching style occasioned by computers are as far-reaching as those that were occasioned by Gutenberg—printed books revolutionized medieval education. Nor does this book deal with issues of changes in curriculum content and presentation. These are all left to professional educators.

The change in classroom technology is an inexorable evolution driven by forces beyond the control of the educational establishment. By recognizing the direction and implications of change, school districts and state governments have an option to shape the future. In doing so they can maximize the benefits of the new technologies while addressing the attendant issues before they become crises.

Computer and communications technologies offer splendid opportunities, new administrative complexities, and a whole lexicon of jargon. Yet the fundamental school issues of educating children remain unchanged: having relevant curricula, capturing students' interest, and adapting to the cognitive styles of a wide range of students. At first, school boards and principals will find that the information age is less about the specifics of technology (which are a moving target) than it is about applying new tools to old problems. Later on, they will find that the technology they have embraced has subtly changed the definition of a school.

Notes

1. However, Bluestein, Colony, and Chowdhury (1994) estimated that only 20% of the households had a personal computer.

2. Rose also notes that the wage premium for college graduates using a computer at work is 30%.

3. Armstrong's book is based on Howard Gardner's (1993) theories first described in his seminal work *Frames of Mind: The Theory of Multiple Intelligences*. Armstrong accepts Gardner's theory of multiple types of intelligence and translates them into classroom settings and recommendations tuned to different cognitive strengths.

4. The report states that 28.8% of the 9th-grade class failed to graduate with their classmates. It is noteworthy that the U.S. Department of Education, National Center for Education Statistics (1993) reports that about 40% of the dropouts between the 10th and 12th grades gave not liking school or failing school as one reason for leaving school.

5. The U.S. Department of Education (1994) reports that 5.25% of children ages 6 to 17 enrolled in schools have "specific learning disabilities" and that 97% of them are in the regular schools. The report goes on to say that only 50% of children ages 14 and older who have a specific learning disability leave school with a diploma.

About the Author

Charles H. McCain is President of McCain Consulting, Inc. and lives in Big Canoe, Georgia. McCain is a consultant, lecturer, and author on the use of computers in schools. His firm's corporate clients range from *Fortune* 500 companies to small businesses. Prior to moving to Georgia, McCain was with Xerox Corporation, where his management responsibilities included information systems development, data-processing centers, long-range planning, and office automation. He also consulted in the areas of corporate acquisitions, product development, and technology assessment.

McCain was one of the founders and the Board of Trustees President of The Norman Howard School, the benchmark school for learning disabled children in New York State. He now serves as Director of Vocational Transitions, Inc., a nonprofit organization devoted to occupational training for disabled people.

He is an arbitrator certified by the American Arbitration Association, a certified computer professional, and a Commander (retired) in the Naval Reserve. His professional affiliations include the Association for Computing Machinery and the Institute for Electrical and Electronic Engineers. A graduate of Washington & Lee University and General Electric's Financial Management Training Program, he and his wife, Ardis, have five children and four grandchildren.

CHAPTER 1

Planning and Management

SYNOPSIS

If the introduction and operation of technology are not managed, they most certainly will be ineffective and unnecessarily expensive. Because the technical revolution will touch every aspect of the school, it will be viewed as threatening by many, and the best of plans may be ignored or subtly sabotaged. A technology planning committee that directly involves all the affected constituencies in the planning process should be considered. Their plans may be more acceptable than those emanating from the front office. Similarly, monitoring the implementation of the plan may be more acceptable and less political if the committee's responsibilities are extended so it oversees the plan's execution.

There are three rules for managing the technology.

1. There must be an overall technical architecture. This architecture describes the major pieces of technology, how they fit together, and how they support the school's goals. It ensures that, even though the implementation will be spread over years, all the components will function together. It is insurance

against the creation of islands of technology that are incapable of useful cooperation.

2. There must be an annual technical planning process. The methodology used is a 5-year supply-demand analysis. It balances the present and future needs of the school against its current technical capabilities to arrive at an unsatisfied demand. Because the unsatisfied demand most certainly will exceed funding resources, the demand is prioritized and the additions to the technology are phased in over 5 years. The first year of the approved 5-year plan is then fleshed out to become the budget for next year; this methodology ensures that activities for next year always are approved in a larger context. Equally important, this methodology directly relates spending to measurable benefits.

3. Finally, there must be a management process that enables administrators to assess both actual spending and benefit realization against the committed plan. Moreover, there must be an annual review that weeds out programs not meeting their stated objectives—this frees resources for more productive programs.

Background

As described in the introduction, the educational system is in the midst of a technical revolution. This most certainly poses a wealth of challenges: significant changes to school facilities, training, technical support, and operational policies. Yet none of these changes can be effected without leadership that is expressed in sound management practices.

Computer-based systems inevitably institutionalize methodologies and processes, and their design and implementation warrant the close attention of school boards and senior officials. Clausewitz, the Prussian military theorist, noted that "war is a continuation of policy by other means." Similarly, computer systems are a continuation of school policy. It is appropriate, therefore, that this first chapter addresses the three key management activities that are essential for success in this venture—technical architecture, planning, and measurements—and how these activities relate to the vision and goals of the school.

Technical Architecture

Few are so foolish or impetuous as to buy windows, doors, and other components for a house without an architectural plan. Yet many schools make substantive investments in computer and communications technology, buildings, and people without a technical architecture (i.e., framework or scheme) to guide them. The probability of the pieces working together to meet the school's educational goals is, at best, small.

In the information systems trade, the word *architecture* is used to describe the overall system in terms of its components and how they fit together to meet the objectives set forth at the outset. The individual components are defined in terms of what function they perform and how they relate to other components as opposed to how the function is performed. Returning to the analogy of the house, the architectural drawings would indicate that the dishwasher is to be installed in the kitchen, under the countertop to the right of the sink, with no mention of how the dishwasher itself is constructed.

An architectural plan is the communications medium between the designer and the prospective owner or user and, finally, between the designer and the builder. It describes how the designer proposes to assemble various components into a final product to satisfy the objectives of the buyer. Once resolved, it communicates what is to be constructed to the builder: what components are required, how they relate to one another, and, most important, what standards will be followed. The architectural emphasis on standards ensures the ability to interchange one piece of hardware with another with similar functions. Once again returning to the house analogy, there are standard dimensions for kitchen counters, and dishwashers have standard electrical and plumbing connections and dimensions. These standards make it possible to swap easily a very basic dishwasher from one manufacturer with a deluxe model from another manufacturer.

In this book, the term *technical architecture* is used to refer to the broad, overarching plan of how the pieces of technology will eventually fit together. Beginning with the goals of the school, the plan addresses not only all the technical elements but also the necessary supporting infrastructure—physical plant, policy, and staffing. It fits all this together as a mosaic to help the school reach its goals. It is both the road map and the rules of the road, ensuring flexibility at the component level while maintaining the integrity of the overall picture. As shown in Figure 1.1, the architecture links the technology and the necessary infrastructure to the school's vision.

If, as Georges Clemenceau suggested, "War is too serious to leave to the generals," then the architectural plan is too important to be left to technical planners. Although technicians and, possibly, generals are necessary, the overall direction and priorities must be controlled by those with broader accountability—senior administrators and the school board. As in any other plan, choices made in the planning process enable certain functions but also tend to limit others; for instance, the choice of a wireless network provides freedom from physical network connections but may preclude multimedia transmissions. For this reason, the school board should insist on a clear, demonstrable linkage between its vision and the elements of the technical architecture.

Beginning with the school board's goals, the architectural planner identifies how technology can support these objectives, what components are necessary, and how the pieces will be linked together. These elements are then refined into standards and policies. The standards define how, for example, a student's computer will communicate with the printer or the library, regardless of the brand names involved. It also sets standards for electric power, air-conditioning, lighting, and even classroom furniture. At another level, the plan also covers organizational needs and policies, including contingency planning, training, and security. In these ways, the architecture establishes the essential building blocks and lays out the ground rules for everything to follow.

It behooves the architectural designer to grasp the stated requirements thoroughly—as well as those not stated. Most people setting forth the requirements have little understanding of the capabilities of present technologies, much less those probable in

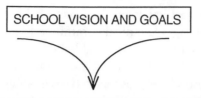

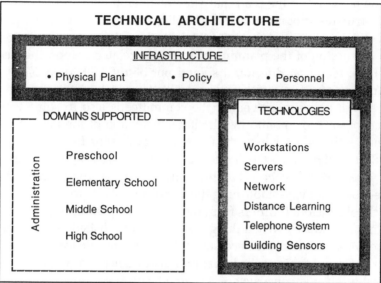

Figure 1.1. Technical Architecture
NOTE: Technical architecture defines an infrastructure that will support the
technology. It ties the technology to the school's vision and goals in terms of
the users' requirements.

the future. The architect, therefore, must be an active participant
in the framing of the requirements, articulating possibilities and
stretching imaginations. The most successful architectural designs will be those most firmly grounded on the community's
future needs, many of which are now only barely perceived.

Planning Process

The latent potential of technology to change every aspect of the
school system induces a tension that elevates planning for tech-

nology to the highest levels of diplomacy. School boards should consider establishing a technical committee to lead the planning process. If such a committee is established, it should include all the affected constituencies in the planning process. Those involved (and those closely associated) will develop a sense of "ownership" of the plan that effectively eliminates many of the destructive "not invented here" feelings that are likely to occur if the plan is seen as the creation of the technical director. Following a discussion of the planning process and related responsibilities of the technical director, it should not be difficult to envision a number of ways a technical committee could lead the planning process. In a similar vein, if the committee is also in some way responsible for monitoring the implementation of the plan, it removes the director from the position of evaluating his or her own efforts and positions the director as a nonpolitical solver of problems.

Creating the technical architecture involves setting a clear direction and then establishing the technical policies to support the school's vision. It differs from the process of planning because it does not address when things will be accomplished, what manpower and dollars are necessary, who is responsible for each task, or, referring again to the house and dishwasher analogy, how the dishwasher is constructed. An architectural document is not a detailed plan for implementing; rather, it is the common starting point for many plans—plans for drawing, piece by piece, the whole picture. It is appropriate that most plans are a consensus reflecting the needs and wishes of the prospective users. Yet when major technical architecture issues are at stake, the consensus process probably should give way to a benevolent dictatorship. The technical issues affecting how all the pieces fit together now and into the 21st century can be exceedingly difficult, and they should be resolved by a leader with sound technical judgment.

The detailed planning processes all take place under the umbrella of the technical architecture. First, a long-range strategy, usually spanning 5 years, is developed. Then, the first year of the strategy is developed further to become a detailed plan for the next year. The acid test of this planning process is the simplicity of the resulting plan—as one wag quipped, "The baroque is worse than the byte."

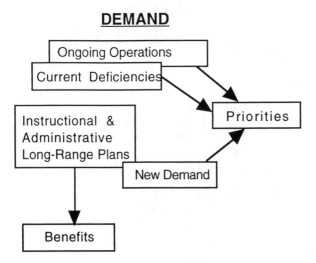

Figure 1.2. The Planning Process—Demand Determination

Annually, the director of technology[1] should lead the long-range technical planning process by bringing together the senior instructional and administrative people. These people must establish the "demand" side of the plan. This delineation of the needs of all potential "customers" (all those who will use the system) is the first step, because customer needs must drive the entire planning process. As shown in Figure 1.2, these needs should be framed in two ways: first, the demands for service that are unmet at the present time, and second, the new demands flowing from the school's instructional and administrative long-range plans. Because the aggregate need most likely will exceed both current and probable future resources, priorities must be set. Because the priorities directly affect the user community, the senior administrators must be directly involved in making these value judgments.

Given an understanding of the customer demand, the technical or "supply" side of the strategy can be assembled. Figure 1.3 depicts how the user priorities are overlaid on the current capabilities. Then, in conjunction with a forecast of how technology will evolve, a migration plan outlines the step-by-step actions that must be taken to evolve from the present state into the new one.

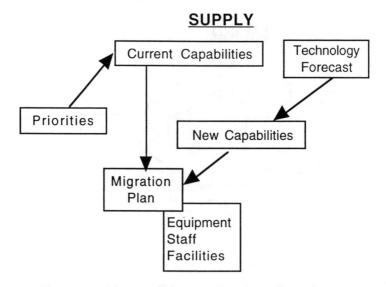

Figure 1.3. The Planning Process—Migration Strategy

As seen in Figure 1.3, the creation of a technical strategy is simply a documentation of a management process, juxtaposing the user community's present and future needs against the capabilities of the present technical environment and new technical capabilities. Schedules of actions required, spending, staffing, and the expected benefits are a natural outgrowth of the process. The completed strategy relates each change in the technical environment to the school's stated needs and provides consistency within the overall technical architecture.

Although Figure 1.2 and Figure 1.4 depict an orderly, more or less sequential process, this is hardly ever the case. Many constituencies, each with their own priorities, are involved, and because resources are constrained, the process tends to be a cyclical one. With patience and nudging, compromises are worked out and a consensus is achieved. One planning director observed, "The process continues until we run out of time and declare a victory."

After the strategy has been accepted, the plans and budget for the ensuing year are simply a refinement of the first year's activities in the 5-year plan. The annual operating plan is a much more

THE PLAN

Figure 1.4. The Planning Process—Plan Preparation

detailed schedule of activities, staffing, and spending; it also fleshes out the rationale for each program, when benefits will be realized, and how the benefits will be measured. As with the 5-year plan, the 1-year operating plan must be approved by the senior administrators and the school board's planning committee. In these review processes, a healthy dose of skepticism is most appropriate; technology projects are particularly susceptible to Murphy's Law. Once launched, project costs are more likely to overrun than underrun the budget, and the anticipated benefits tend to erode or evaporate. Some battle-scarred industry executives have arrived at the following guidelines that, with a change in terminology, are applicable to a school system:

- If the cost recovery point is in the first full year of operation, quickly get on with the project.
- If the cost recovery point is not reached until the second year of operation, make sure the estimates are solid and reasonable contingencies are foreseen.
- If the cost recovery point is in the third year, it is a risky project. There will be many surprises and few will be welcome.

- If the cost recovery point is more than 3 years away, have the project reconfigured into several smaller projects that will have a higher probability of success.

There are three corollaries to these rules. First, do not entertain any project if the end users have not been directly involved in the planning. Second, if a project once launched looks progressively worse—more time, more cost, less benefit—it is on the wrong track. Cut the losses and stop the project. Third, planning is great, but delivery is what counts; do something now that works and improve it later.

Each year, this planning cycle is refreshed: The technical architecture is reviewed; the instructional and administration plans lead to a new, prioritized user-demand case; and the long-range strategy is updated to address the revised demand, which in turn becomes the basis for the next annual plan.

In large school districts, the work of technical planning may require a full-time staff of one or more persons. In more typical situations, it is a responsibility assigned to a senior member of the technical staff or even a task taken on by the technical director.

Measurements

No matter how small a school district may be, sound principles of accounting, measuring, and reporting should be followed.

- Accounting reports must be structured to be useful management tools for those accountable for the program and for management alike.
- Proposals to allocate resources must have their promised benefits framed in terms that can be measured subsequently.
- Much as there must be accountability for expenditures, there must be accountability for achieving the anticipated benefits.

The school district's accounting and expense reporting system should be tuned so that the major cost elements of the technical environment are reported by type of expense and by the organi-

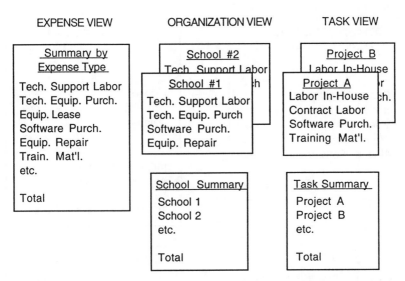

Figure 1.5. Reports Reflecting Accountabilities and Expense Classifications

zation responsible for the expenditure. The system should align reported spending with the way the moneys were budgeted. Also, the system should have the capability of presenting the data from several different points of view. For instance, in Figure 1.5, costs are reported by type of expense, by school, and by task, even though a task may span several schools.

All computer and telecommunications expenses should be reported together to give visibility to opportunities for operational improvements and possible cost savings. At times, this type of aggregation may be inconsistent with traditional school accounting. For instance, it may be appropriate and desirable to classify and report educational software purchases as both instructional material and software. To avoid confusion, when the expense is shown in the secondary report, it should be flagged as a memorandum item. Often, these are shown "below the line" as indirect expenses after the direct expenses are totaled, as in Figure 1.6.

Useful accounting reports must not only reflect actual spending but also relate this spending to the budget for the current month, year-to-date, and, for multiyear projects, project-to-date. Of course,

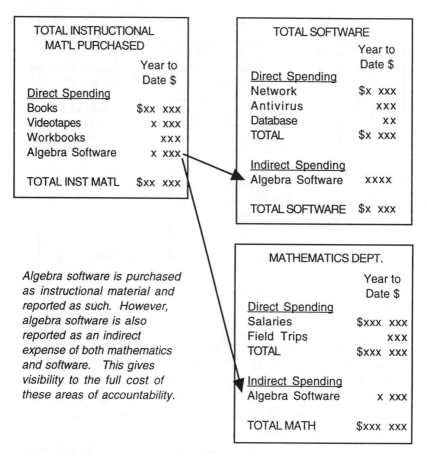

Figure 1.6. Expenses Reported as Both Direct and Indirect Spending

NOTE: Algebra software is purchased as instructional material and reported as such. However, algebra software also is reported as an indirect expense of both mathematics and software. This gives visibility to the full cost of these areas of accountability.

project plans and the 1-year operating plan also should be developed at the same level of detail as the costs will be reported. Planning at a very detailed level is a substantial effort; a balance must be struck between the cost of developing and maintaining detailed input to the planning and accounting systems and the management value received from more detailed reports.

There is a truism—if you can't measure it, you can't improve it. The school board's policy should be that investments in technology directly relate to the objectives of the school system, and those who propose these investments must be accountable for the benefits promised. If a worthwhile assessment of technology investments is to be made, the foundations for measurement must be laid in the planning process, and the mechanisms to capture the data for subsequent evaluation must be part of that plan.

Any proposal to invest in technology must be supported by a concrete description of the anticipated benefits, and unquantified benefits should be challenged. Even when the benefit cannot be measured directly, the effects of the change often can be assessed indirectly; for instance, improved truancy statistics or attitude surveys may indicate the success of the program. Whenever a proposal is rationalized by the promise of a measurable change, the plan must include these elements:

- A measurement of the present situation
- A means to collect the data measuring the change
- A commitment to report the results

This is not to say all proposals without quantifiable benefits should be rejected. The suggested emphasis here on benefits and their measurement is to reinforce a mind-set: Investments in technology must relate to the objectives of the school system, and people must be held accountable for the benefits promised.

School officials must actively manage their investment in technology programs; their management process should capitalize on the successes and kill the failures. A deliberate annual assessment is essential. Using the success criteria established in each program's plans, the projects are ranked by performance in respect to both cost and benefits. The top third are considered for expansion; the middle third, perhaps, are given a second chance; and the bottom third are terminated. Unmanaged, programs easily can become institutionalized regardless of benefits realized or not realized. Worse, the resources consumed by unproductive programs could otherwise be applied to new, promising ideas. It is often more difficult to stop an ill-conceived program than it is to start a well-conceived one. The president of a school board in a northeastern city once observed that the value of a program often seemed to be inversely proportional to its complexity and cost.

Note

1. The director of technology has overall responsibility for all computers, software, and telecommunications within a school district. Job descriptions of this and related positions are included in Appendix C.

CHAPTER 2

Designing the Physical Plant

SYNOPSIS

As noted previously, an underlying assumption in this book is that within a decade, computer and communications technology will saturate most schools. Saturation means that there will be a computer on every desk, and each computer will be linked to a network within the school that connects to networks beyond the school. When schools contemplate new buildings or major renovations, they should anticipate this saturation. If plans make provisions for what is to come, small investments at the outset can preclude expensive changes later.

Many schools have installed several computers in the classroom successfully. This experience, however, can be misleading when planning for the construction of new school buildings or the renovation of older buildings. Computers have a number of characteristics that impose significant demands on the school's physical plant:

- Take up space
- Emit electromagnetic radiation

- Create ergonomic stress
- Connect to networks
- Use electricity
- Generate heat

The consequences of these factors are far-reaching; some of the more striking are noted below.

Computers Take Up Space. The typical desk or tablet armchair is no longer adequate. Desks must have space not only for the processor, monitor, keyboard, and mouse but also for textbooks, paper, and pencils. As the size of the desks increases by a factor of three or more, the dimensions of the classroom also must increase. The typical classroom size will increase from about 750 square feet to approximately 1,000 square feet—a 33% change.

In addition to larger classrooms, there are other new requirements for space: larger wiring closets and space for centralized equipment, storage, and technical staff offices.

Ergonomic Stress. Keyboards bring with them the risk of repetitive stress injuries, for example, carpal tunnel syndrome. Classroom desks must be designed specifically for keyboard use. Improper lighting leads to reflections and glare on monitors, and this leads to eye discomfort. Both classroom artificial and natural light sources must be controlled to eliminate reflections on the cathode ray tube (CRT).

Electricity. Nameplate data on the current generation of desktop machines indicate a current draw of about six or seven amperes, indicating one circuit for every two or three machines. Although nameplate data almost always overstate power requirements, the clear trend is for new equipment to require more power than that which it displaces. It is certain that older buildings must be rewired and new buildings constructed to new standards. However, the problem is also one of how to deliver the power to each desk. There are a number classroom wiring methods, but, at least in new construction, a raised-floor system may provide the best balance of initial cost, maintenance cost, and flexibility. In renovations, a number of other options are available and discussed in the main text.

Computers are particularly susceptible to electrical disturbances. Spikes, surges, sags, and other anomalies can damage equipment, corrupt data, and disrupt operations. The school must provide all equipment with power purged of these happenings; in addition, critical equipment may need a source of power not subject to power outages.

Electromagnetic Radiation. Radiation from CRT monitors has been identified by some as a cause of cancer and, possibly, birth defects. There is equally persuasive proof that this is not the case. In the face of ambiguity and potential negligence suits, schools should buy low-radiation monitors and keep users at least 20 inches away from monitors.

Network Connection. In addition to an electrical connection at each desk, there must be a connection to the building network. The solution to the classroom electrical distribution problem also must be suitable for network wiring.

A high bandwidth (capacity) network is needed to support multimedia computer applications that will be used in the classrooms. It requires special wiring and specialized electronic switching equipment that have a variety of names, including *hubs, routers, bridges,* and *repeaters.* The design of the network must be tailored to the present and future needs of the school, and the specifications for its installation must satisfy not only local building codes but also American National Standards Institute (ANSI) standards. The services of both a network design consultant and a professional engineer are an excellent investment.

The electrical and communication wires emanating from the classroom lead to a wiring closet. The recommended space for a wiring closet is 110 square feet per 100 computers. This closet should be close to the computers, which may be a problem in older schools.

Heating, Ventilation, and Air-Conditioning. Most of the electrical energy consumed by a computer is converted into heat energy and dissipated into the room. A room with 25 computers will require an additional two or three tons of air-conditioning. Also, because the computers may not always be operational, each classroom must control its own air-conditioning.

Background

The life span of a new school building is about 50 years, and the useful life of a major renovation is half that. When investments are made in the physical plant, they must accommodate not only the technologies now in use but also those that are anticipated within the next 25 years.

The following is a risk-free assumption: Within the life span of any major school construction or renovation now undertaken, computers will have saturated the classroom. In other words, a computer will be dedicated to each teacher and each student in every classroom. All of these machines will be interconnected by a network extending beyond the boundaries of the school building. Teachers and students alike will access all of the network capabilities from their homes, which will become extensions of the school system. As will be discussed, this technology saturation has significant implications for the design of school buildings and their furnishings.

The electronic school will not happen instantly, because the existing investment in plant and personnel skills cannot be changed overnight. Not only is an instant transformation unaffordable, but it would be unwise, because much is yet to be learned about how best to use the new technologies. An evolutionary approach is called for—an open-ended strategy of incremental steps that build on one another while providing ample opportunity for midcourse corrections.

Schools and classrooms will evolve through a number of interim phases as computers move into the classroom and teachers capitalize on them. The following examples represent the more obvious transitional states, but they are not necessarily sequential steps.

1. The computers are in a school computer laboratory supervised by a computer specialist. They are networked to several printers in the laboratory, but the network does not extend beyond the laboratory walls. There is no direct connection between students' use of the machines and classroom subject matter.

2. The computers are in a laboratory dedicated to one discipline and shared by several teachers (e.g., four or five English teachers). Use of the machines is directly related to the lesson plans, and student use is supervised by the responsible teacher.

3. A classroom has several computers arranged in clusters or on the periphery of the room. The machines are in a separate area of the classroom, and the principal instructional mode is still the traditional lecture, working with textbooks and workbooks.

4. A. Computers are on teachers' desks to support administrative tasks and some preparatory tasks such as lesson plans, test development, and transparency making.

   B. The computers on teachers' desks are tied to a schoolwide network providing access to shared printers and databases. There is instant access to the likes of event calendars and the paperless, electronic submission of classroom attendance and other reports to the administration office.

5. Some students and teachers access school computer facilities such as the library, electronic bulletin boards, and electronic mailboxes from home computers via the telephone network and modem.

6. A technical staff is in place to manage technology projects, maintain equipment and software, and train, coach, and assist the users. School policies consider the issues incident to the new technologies.

As a school moves through the above stages, computer and telecommunications technologies will impose new requirements on every aspect of the school building. Classroom technology, the furniture and its layout, lighting, electrical and communications

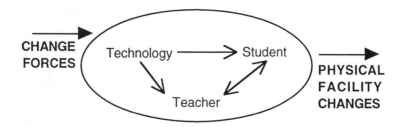

Figure 2.1. Change in Education Driving Changes in the Physical Plant

wiring, and heating, ventilation, and air-conditioning are all interrelated. Changes to one element often must be balanced by modifications in several other elements (see Figure 2.1). Although the following discussion considers them individually, they must, finally, be dealt with as a whole.

Decision makers who decide to ignore the implications of the electronic age in the design of their buildings are making a decision for early obsolescence. When investments in the physical plant are contemplated, the requirements of the anticipated technology must be an integral part of the specifications given to the architects and engineers. Many of the recommendations in this chapter can be made at little or no additional cost when a new building is in the design stage, but they will be very expensive after the structure has been completed. Other suggestions are well suited to retrofitting older buildings.

For planners with less than perfect foresight, there are four keys to success:

- Design for the greatest degree of flexibility.
- Build the physical infrastructure when it can be done most economically; for example, installing larger-size conduits costs very little in the construction stage and would be expensive to change after the building is completed.
- Defer implementing details until they are necessary; for example, when a building is under construction, the main electrical and communications wiring should be installed,

but wiring individual rooms could be deferred until the equipment installation is more imminent.

• Planners should adhere to widely accepted industry and national standards, such as those published by the American National Standards Institute (ANSI). Standards offer the best assurance of flexibility.

In summary, design for flexibility, build when it is most economical, defer the details, and conform to standards.

This chapter explores the physical implications of computer saturation: Virtually every aspect of the physical plant will be different from pre-1990 structures. Undoubtedly, new school construction will test the ingenuity of planners, architects, and engineers for some years to come as they address the varied elements that support this new technology. On the other hand, the problems of building a new school are dwarfed by the difficulty of adapting older buildings. Few of these structures were designed for ease of modification, and their renovation will pose significant engineering and architectural challenges to school officials.

Financing the modifications to buildings built before the electronics age may prove to be just as difficult as resolving the structural issues themselves. Bond referendums for new schools are relatively easy to justify to the community; population growth and temporary classrooms in the school yard are self-evident. By contrast, the cost of renovating existing buildings to accommodate new technology is harder to rationalize; most of the deficiencies are invisible. Besides, the relative ease with which people have installed a single PC in their homes leads them to underestimate grossly the complexities of preparing a building for hundreds or thousands of computers.

School boards must gain wide public support for the expense of updating buildings and facilities. The program requires a well-executed public information campaign that directly relates computer and communications technology to students' successful preparation for the job market or further schooling. Although many constituents already may be true believers, the broad consensus required for major spending cannot be achieved without public education.

Renovating older buildings poses unique challenges, but the ingredients of success are the same as for new construction:

- A clear statement of what benefits are expected from the technology
- A comprehensive long-range plan for computer and communications technology, including building retrofits and a strategy for financing them
- A technical architecture to establish how the pieces of technology will fit together
- A public information program

Without these elements, the inevitable cobbled fixes ultimately will prove both unsatisfactory and costly. This is not to say that interim solutions are imprudent; rather, they should be undertaken in the context of an overall plan.

Classroom

Classroom Size

Well within the next decade every student's desk will need space for a computer monitor, keyboard, and mouse or other pointing device.[1] These machines will not displace books, pencils, and paper so much as richly supplement them. The implication is clear: The size of the student desktop must be doubled or tripled to accommodate this hardware. Not only will each student require more space, but the teacher's work space also must be enlarged. Indeed, the Georgia Department of Education (1994) suggests 30 to 40 square feet of space for each workstation—a space that includes a table, chair, and circulation area. In addition, classroom space is needed for printers, scanners, network equipment, and a large-screen projector tied to the teacher's machine. The needed increase in space, depending on how the classroom is configured, could be 30% or perhaps even more. The typical room size of 750 square feet for 25 students today may need to be

1,000 square feet. Of course, if classroom dimensions cannot be changed, classes must have fewer students.

The key variable in the desk space required for each student is the size of the monitor. At present, most CRT displays have 14-inch or 15-inch (measured diagonally) viewing surfaces, but the trend is toward larger 17-inch displays that can show a full page at a time. In classrooms devoted to art, drafting, or other subjects requiring still larger displays, a commensurate increase in space per student is necessary.

Lighting

If computer usage in a classroom is intensive, as it will be at times, great care must be given to the source of ambient light. Glare, low-image contrast, and stray reflections on a computer display tremendously affect one's ability to use the equipment without eyestrain and associated fatigue. Indeed, in one study, 47% of office workers complained of eyestrain; it was the most frequently mentioned complaint and no doubt partly attributable to improper lighting (Steelcase, 1991a).

In classrooms, ceiling lights are often a source of glare and reflection on the displays (Rea, 1991).[2] Bright lights should not be placed behind or above the user. The ceiling should be evenly lit without the bright spots caused by most ceiling lights. One way to achieve better ceiling illumination is to replace existent ceiling fluorescent light fixtures with fixtures incorporating a compound parabolic louver design. In classrooms with ceiling heights of at least 9.5 feet, indirect lighting fixtures suspended from the ceiling are suitable if the application requires no more than 500 lux (approximately 50 foot-candles) or if supplementary task lighting is provided.

The overall light level in the classroom must be controllable: Low-light levels are needed for video presentations and use of desktop machines, whereas light levels in the 450 to 800 lux range (approximately 40 to 75 foot-candles) are typical for textbook and writing work. Classroom lights should be controlled by two or more dimmers so that lights at the front of the room can be set very low to enhance the images on large-screen displays. In many cases, inexpensive, individual task lights on the desks will enable an overall reduction in room light level and also cut energy costs.

Sunlight (10,000 to 100,000 lux) streaming through windows is much more intense and distracting than artificial lighting. Monitors should be at a right angle to any window so the window light is neither reflected off the display nor is a backdrop to the monitor—a brightly lit backdrop reduces the apparent contrast on the display and increases eyestrain. Designers should strive for a glare-free classroom yet provide some visual access to the outside; rooms without windows will require two doors. In existing buildings, light-blocking window drapes are the most economical solution. When glare and reflections cannot be ameliorated, antiglare screens can be attached to the front of the monitor but should be considered only as a last resort, because they typically reduce the brightness of the image by 50% or more.[3]

Although medical research has found no correlation between the use of computer monitors and eye disease (American Academy of Ophthalmology, 1992; Bardelli, Cavara, & Bietti, 1989),[4] eyestrain is a frequent complaint when computer monitors are used for protracted periods. Intensive use of computers can engender visual problems and excerbate others heretofore unnoticed. Even if the monitors are in ideal surroundings, some people will complain of eyestrain. These students and employees should be advised to have an eye examination. Even those with newly fitted reading glasses may experience difficulties because the monitor is set beyond the distance where the eyeglasses are designed to focus. Many requiring glasses for reading will need another pair for working at a computer. In addition, intensive work at a computer monitor tends to reduce a person's blink rate; this dries the eyes and gives rise to complaints of eye irritation.

Whatever the cause, eyestrain can be reduced significantly if, every half hour or so, there is a visual respite to let eye muscles relax by focusing on more distant objects.

Furniture and Fixtures

Much of the classroom furniture in use today would look familiar to Rip Van Winkle. Classroom technology—books, blackboards, pencils, and paper—has not changed significantly in over a century. Now, however, a number of factors call for new and different furniture and fixtures; the most significant factors are discussed below.

- Keyboards need to be several inches lower than typical work surfaces. Key tops should be level with the bottom of the bent elbow of a seated person. Most adults will find a shelf 27 inches from the floor places the keyboard properly. Intensive use of keyboards at the usual 30-inch desktop height is a major contributor to carpal tunnel syndrome and other painfully incapacitating repetitive stress injuries, some of which require surgery. The National Institute of Occupational Safety and Health studies show that more than 20% of employees who primarily work with computers are affected by repetitive stress injuries. Stephanie Brown's (1993) *Preventing Computer Injury: The Handbook* is a well-illustrated tutorial on avoiding keyboard injuries and retraining those who are already injured. Yet it is noteworthy that in spite of anecdotal evidence, lawsuits to recover damages attributable to repetitive stress injury have been remarkably unsuccessful. *Carolyn Burst v. Apple Computer* (1995) was reported by *Datamation* (1995) as the sixth repetitive stress injury case to go to trial in 2 years; in each instance the plaintiff lost.

- Many experts recommend that classroom computer monitors be placed below the line of sight in the usual reading position for a book on the desk. In other words, the viewing surface should be flat, or almost flat, on the desktop—a position more suitable for students making frequent reference to the keyboard and to desktop material. Note that this is different from the monitor placement recommended for stenographers and data-entry clerks; their work and their expert keyboard skills argue that the monitor should be about 10 degrees below the horizontal line of sight.

- Student desks must accommodate a computer monitor, keyboard, and mouse or other pointer and still have space for an open textbook and a writing surface. The height of the desk seat needs to be adjustable to place taller or shorter students in a position to use the keyboard properly.

- A computer and a CRT monitor can weigh 30, 50, or more pounds. Tables and desks must be constructed to support this load. Unless properly reinforced, tables made of medium-density fiberboard (MDF) and plastic laminates will sag under the weight of several machines.

- All the computers in the classroom must be connected both to electric power and to the classroom network. These connection points must be convenient to each desk, and the connectors need to be sufficiently rugged to withstand classroom wear and tear.

- Provision must be made to accommodate equipment such as printers, scanners, network hubs, electric power conditioners, and computer supplies in each classroom. Cables and other support equipment create a distracting and unattractive visual clutter if they are not properly placed and housed.

- Dust can damage computers, and whiteboards should be installed in place of blackboards. These whiteboards will be supplemented by a large computer monitor or other projection system tied to the teacher's computer. The viewing surface must be large enough and positioned so that even textual material can be read easily from any position in the classroom.

The need for investments in appropriate furniture must not be overlooked because these furnishings markedly affect how well teachers and students will interact with the technology. Also, the design of furniture and fixtures affects how well the equipment functions and how easily it can be serviced. In the next section, a number of possible classroom configurations, each requiring furniture probably not presently in the classroom, is discussed.

Room Layout and Desks

Research projects using actual classroom conditions have developed no single ideal classroom layout for teaching with the aid of computers. Not surprisingly, the Apple Classroom of Tomorrow Research Project (Stuebing, Knox, Petrakaki, & Giddings, 1991) noted the following factors as significantly affecting classroom layout: grade level, building structure, class size, and equipment. Subject matter and the specific assignment had a significant bearing on the layout: A math assignment required a computer for each student, whereas science experiments were often best done with several students using a single machine. Teaching style was also a determinant of the layout. Although no standards have evolved, a number of basic layouts (and numerous variations on them) have been found useful.

The layout of the classroom and the design of the furniture must be considered together. In the following pages, a number of classroom and furniture design options are discussed. Some are only appropriate for new construction or major renovations, but others are well suited to existing buildings. In any case, they should all be viewed as starting points for crafting solutions to best satisfy specific situations and preserve flexibility.

One innovative student desk design places a conventional CRT display beneath a nonreflective window in the desktop, provides a lowered surface for the keyboard, and has a conventional-height writing surface (see Figure 2.2). The monitor is placed in a position that some consider ideal for viewing (Chaffin, 1991),[5] and it no longer interferes with the student's view of the teacher and whiteboard. The keyboard is positioned to reduce fatigue and wrist injury. The processor is positioned out of the way on a shelf under the desk. With this type of desk, the only element constraining the furniture arrangement is access to a power source and the network. Also, the keyboard slides out of the way so that the entire desk becomes an unencumbered work surface.

The economic argument for this type of desk is that it conserves classroom space; this translates into lower construction and operating costs. This particular desk design, however, requires special care with room lighting, because even with nonglare glass, the horizontal display is prone to glare from overhead lighting, and sometimes antiglare hoods are necessary.

Another type of desk (Figure 2.3) also combines the computer with the writing surface but uses a freestanding vertical monitor.

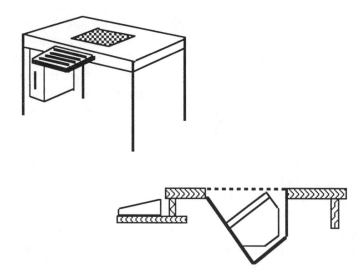

Figure 2.2. Keyboard, Embedded Display, and Writing Surface Combined

Although the monitor is not in the ideal horizontal position, the display surface is less subject to glare and stray reflections from overhead lights than the embedded monitor. It can be assembled by school maintenance personnel with standard tables and readily available keyboard trays; moreover, the keyboard tray can be

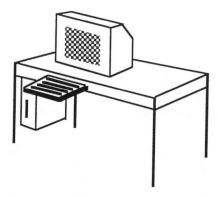

Figure 2.3. Keyboard, Freestanding Display, and Writing Surface

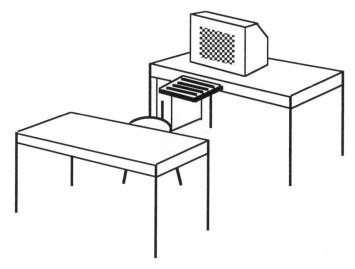

Figure 2.4. Separate Work Surfaces for Computing and Writing

easily relocated to accommodate left-handed students. The principle advantage of a monitor on the desktop is that it facilitates use of a single machine by several students collaborating on a project.

In this configuration, as well as in the following one, the student's seating position must change depending on whether the task involves working on the computer or using a textbook and handwriting. The need to shift positions argues for chairs or stools with casters.

A third option (Figure 2.4) provides for both computing and writing surfaces but places them in a line instead of on a single surface as in the two previous examples. When the teacher is lecturing or demonstrating, the students use the writing surface and face the "front" of the classroom. When using the computer, they turn around and face the "rear" of the room. In the Apple Classroom of Tomorrow research, some teachers liked this arrangement because they could more easily see what was happening on the students' monitors.

In situations in which the clutter of desktop monitors is an impediment to teacher-student interaction, the teacher could be

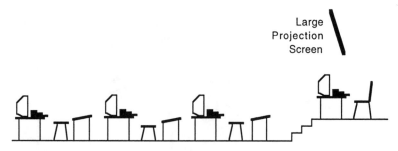

Figure 2.5. Classroom With Teacher Podium

placed on a podium, or the student desks even could be stair-stepped, as in an amphitheater (see Figure 2.5).

Where underfloor wiring access is impractical for each desk and power poles from the desk to the ceiling are unacceptable, the arrangement in Figure 2.6 should be considered. Each paired row of desks is served by conduits and outlets on the floor. Although

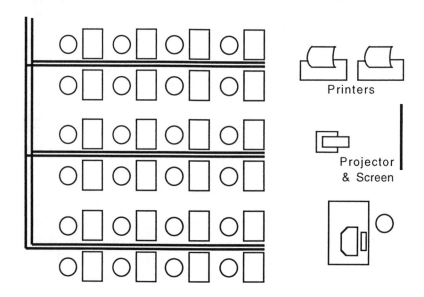

Figure 2.6. Power and Communications Conduit Shared by Paired Rows of Desks

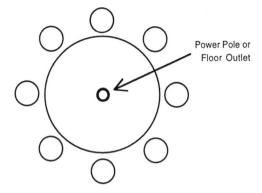

Figure 2.7. Cluster of Eight Workstations

two conduits are illustrated, only a single conduit is necessary if a fiber-optic cable is used for the network.

All of the preceding schemes are appropriate for classrooms in which each student has a computer and the activity is a mix of work on the computer, traditional desk work, lectures, and teacher-led demonstrations.

Instances arise, such as in the lower grades, in which only a few students in a class require a computer at one time. In this case a computer cluster, as shown in Figure 2.7, may be the best solution. Clusters are also well suited to computer laboratories and in libraries, where all the students' time is spent at their computers and there is no lecture-style teaching.

The layouts using clustered workstations are particularly well suited to older buildings, because network and power connections for a number of machines can be provided by a single set of floor outlets or a power pole from each cluster to the ceiling.

Clustered machines have several disadvantages. First, it is difficult for the teacher to keep track of what is happening; second, some students at a cluster cannot see the teacher easily. Third, unless windows have light-proof coverings, some of the students will face bright windows, and others will have window light reflecting off the display.

The last alternative (Figure 2.8) is an array of machines along the wall of the classroom. This option is only suitable when a few

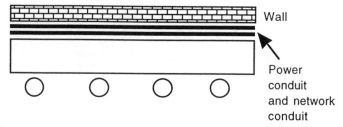

Figure 2.8. Workstations Facing a Wall

machines are added to an existent classroom. The wiring is simple and it requires few other changes in the room layout. The distinguishing drawbacks are: first, it is suitable for only a small number of machines, and second, students must face the wall. Nevertheless, with foresight, this can be a stepping-stone to the configuration of paired rows of desks discussed earlier.

Electromagnetic Radiation

In the industrialized world we are inescapably surrounded by electromagnetic fields (EMF). Electric wiring in walls, electric blankets, high-voltage power lines, and electric shavers are all sources of EMF. These magnetic fields are described by frequency, measured in cycles per second or Herz (Hz), and field strength is measured in milligauss (mG).

Since computer terminals with CRT displays first became prevalent, a continuing discussion about their effect on the health of users has swirled through the press here and abroad. It often has been difficult to understand the facts because much of what has been published has been to buttress a political argument, been sensationalized by the press, or, as one researcher put it, is bad data and sham science. As with other poorly understood potential health threats, myths about electromagnetic radiation abound. *U.S. News and World Report* noted four myths that it found particularly prevalent ("Computer Waves," 1990):

- Small displays always have less magnetic radiation than large displays. (Rather than size, EMF is a function of the CRT tube angle; a deep tube with a narrow angle will have a weaker field than a shallow, wide-angle tube.)

- EMF fields from older monitors are less intense than those from newer ones. (Displays now available with MPR II and TCO ratings have much less radiation.)
- Magnetic radiation is blocked by mesh antiglare screens. (Only solid materials with magnetic properties, such as iron, can block the EMF.)
- Turning down the display brightness reduces magnetic radiation danger. (False.)

Many of the health concerns surrounding desktop electronics in the 1970s have been proven to be without substance. Others, such as eyestrain and carpal tunnel syndrome, have been thoroughly researched, and the preventive measures are generally understood and easily implemented. Electromagnetic radiation, however, still remains an open issue for two reasons.

- First, there is measurable radiation from CRT displays (be they computers or television sets), and some researchers have developed statistical evidence pointing to EMF as a source of cancer—particularly in children. Some laboratory studies have demonstrated that animal cells respond to magnetic fields, but only at very specific frequencies and intensity—at slightly higher or lower intensities, for instance, there may be no response. Many of these experiments, however, have yet to pass the basic test of scientific validity—replication in another laboratory. Moreover, hard evidence linking these and other laboratory experiments to humans has not been developed yet.
- Second, even if some credence is given to the statistical and laboratory research reports, there is no consensus as to how much radiation is too much. On the other hand, in 1994, Washington State's Department of Labor and Industry declared that a worker was entitled to compensation for cancer that he claimed was caused by exposure to EMF at work. The *Wall Street Journal* noted that this may be the first time a government

agency has acknowledged a causal relationship (Richards, 1994). With two apparently irreconcilable camps of scientific opinion as to the health threat of EMF, school administrators are left in a quandary. In the face of this ambiguity, it is prudent to take two basic precautions that involve little cost.

Purchase Specifications. CRTs generate two types of magnetic fields: ELF (extra-low frequency) 60 Hz radiation from the power transformer and VLF (very low frequency) radiation from the deflection coils at the rear of the CRT. Sweden's Board for Measurements and Testing has developed standards establishing safe levels of ELF and VLF emissions. These standards are widely accepted in industrial nations.

The older standard, MPR II, is the one most often cited by manufacturers. It states ELF should be no more than 2.5 mG at any point 19.7 inches from the machine. The newer TCO'92 standard[6] is more stringent, especially on emissions from the front of the monitor, where the measurements are to be made 11.8 inches from the monitor. In addition, TCO'92 sets stricter energy consumption standards. A number of manufacturers are now making monitors to the MPR II standard, and a few are adhering to the TCO'92 standard. Schools desiring to minimize the risk of magnetic radiation should opt for monitors meeting at least the MPR II standard.

Machine Spacing. Because few schools have EMF meters, a reasonable approach is to follow the recommendation of the International Labour Organization (1994): Position the monitor at least as far from other persons as it is from the operator. Although this does not constrain side-to-side spacing, it requires that there should be about 20 inches between the back of a student and the display behind him or her. This is illustrated in Figure 2.9.

One way to increase the distance between students and the machines behind them is to stagger the rows of desks. Another option, a variation of the paired-rows scheme mentioned earlier, is to have the desks face one another as in Figure 2.10. This arrangement provides ample spacing between students. Although

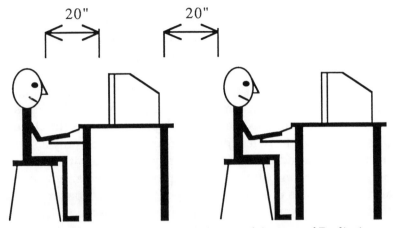

Figure 2.9. Spacing Between Student and Source of Radiation

the desks are not oriented toward the front of the classroom, it is suitable for a computer laboratory.

Field strength falls off dramatically as the source of radiation is moved away. Indeed, the single most effective EMF shield is distance. (The field strength decreases with the square of the distance—at 20 inches the radiation will be one quarter of the strength than at 10 inches and one eighth that at 5 inches).

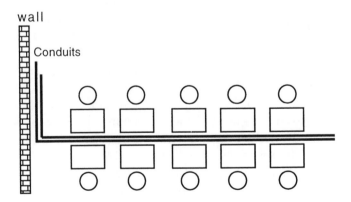

Figure 2.10. Paired Row of Desks Facing Each Other to Reduce Radiation Exposure

None of these recommendations guarantee that there will not be a claim of EMF-related illness; however, responsible actions can be taken in the face of a still ambiguous threat. Moreover, these recommendations are a plausible defense against negligence in the event of legal action brought by the parents of a student diagnosed with some malignancy or inexplicable illness.

To conclude with good news, liquid crystal displays (LCD) and plasma displays have less power consumption and only a small fraction of the radiation of CRT displays. At present, LCD displays are seen on battery-driven laptop computers, where the additional cost is rationalized by their low-power consumption. Plasma displays are in limited production for use in specialized applications. As the technology improves and manufacturing volumes increase, non-CRT displays will become competitive with CRT displays in some parts of the desktop machine market; however, it is not clear when these flat, low-emission displays will be economically practical for classroom use.

Electrical System

Power Distribution

Depending on advancements in battery and display technologies, battery-operated portable computers might possibly be suitable for student use within the next decade or so. Curriculum and school policy permitting, students might carry their own battery-operated computer with them and attach it to the network at their desk in each classroom. In that case, of course, the need for electric power outlets at student desks could be eliminated. Although battery-operated machines suited to classroom use are a possibility, their existence is not sufficiently ensured to warrant school designs predicated on them. Therefore, planners should assume that every device in the classroom will require a convenient electrical outlet as well as one for the network.

If machines are located along classroom walls, they can be easily served from conduits mounted on the wall with outlets about every four feet. If machines are arranged in clusters, each

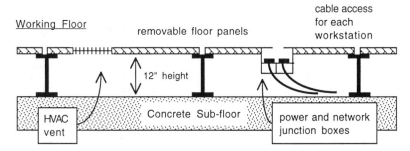

Figure 2.11. Raised Floor for Power and Network Access and for Air-Conditioned Movement (Plenum)

cluster can be served by a power pole from the ceiling or from floor outlets.

When each student has a computer on his or her desk, however, power and communications outlets must be built into every desk or be readily accessible to each desk. If power poles are an unacceptable visual clutter, then floor-level electrical and communications wiring must be used in a way that does not impede classroom traffic. The three basic approaches are the following:

- Covered wiring troughs are embedded in the concrete floor, and if the troughs are spaced three feet apart,[7] access for any furniture configuration is ensured. This type of floor usually is covered with carpet laid in small squares for easy access to the troughs. These troughs, however, are feasible only in new construction.

- A second approach is a raised-floor system, as illustrated in Figure 2.11. A raised floor offers greater flexibility than troughs, and wiring changes are easier to make. It is well suited to new construction. Even in existent buildings, it is the preferred approach in selected areas such as the school's central equipment rooms and data-processing centers. Industry and some schools have found that the greater initial construction cost of a raised floor is more than offset by reduced service expense and subsequent costs of technical and classroom changes. In

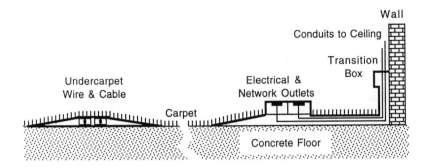

Figure 2.12. Power and Network Access With Undercarpet Wiring

Figure 2.11, the 12-inch elevation over the subfloor accommodates heating and cooling (HVAC) ducts as well as power and communications wiring. It is particularly well suited to central equipment rooms.

- Another type of raised flooring, only 3 inches high, is well suited to classrooms and can be installed over existing floors in older buildings. Although its height does not accommodate the HVAC, it does provide flexibility and easy access to communications and power connections for desktop electronics.

- The third option, illustrated in Figure 2.12, is undercarpet wiring. It is designed for installation in existing buildings and has a lower initial cost than a raised floor. The wires are run through almost flat plastic raceways that make a barely perceptible bump in the carpet. Undercarpet wiring, of course, requires carpeting laid in squares at some additional initial cost over carpet laid from rolls. Yet in existing schools, where permissible under state and local codes, undercarpet wiring with carpet laid in squares may be a low-cost and flexible way to deliver power and communications to each desk in a classroom or office.

As schools install classroom electronics, they will soon develop a maze of wires, cables, and sundry components. To diagnose and repair wiring problems, one must keep accurate records of all power and communications wiring. Some office buildings have lost control of their wiring layout and have therefore accumulated miles of unusable cable above the ceilings and below the floors. In some instances, all the wiring has had to be removed and a fresh start made. Maintenance personnel and contractors must be required to provide the school with "as-built" wiring diagrams noting every outlet and the path of every wire.

Equipment Power Requirements

Each piece of electronic equipment inevitably increases the total demand for power in the building. The electric power consumed by electronic devices is mostly converted to heat energy, which must be handled by the HVAC system at some further increase in power demand.[8]

If a classroom consists of 25 computers (24 students plus a teacher) plus three printers, the power requirement is 14,000 watts or more.[9] If larger monitors or other equipment such as classroom projectors are used, the demand further increases. This demand for electric current is especially dramatic when put in context: Other than lighting, many classrooms at present may occasionally only use 500 watts for an overhead projector or even less for a TV or VCR.

The plight of a well-known corporation is an object lesson. In the early 1980s, the corporation, seeking to relocate its regional office, bought a new 13-story office building. Before the corporation's office workers had filled half of the building, executives were dismayed to find that all of the building's electrical power and air-conditioning capacity had been consumed. The engineering standards used in the building design did not anticipate a computer on every desk. Before the corporation could complete its occupancy, it had to undertake costly changes. Had these requirements been included in the original specifications for the building, the added cost would have been a small fraction of the cost of the changes made later.

Manufacturers recently have addressed one aspect of the power problem by introducing "green machines" that shift into a low-power mode when they are idle. Where machines remain powered up but are just used intermittently, this mode will reduce total power consumption. However, because it does not reduce the power when the machine is active, peak power demand remains unchanged.

Although the power requirements of some types of individual electronic components will continue to decrease, most researchers in the field believe the power consumption of most desktop computers units will not diminish. They believe demands placed by more complex applications, friendlier user interfaces, and multimedia (sound and video) will require faster machines with much more memory and a vastly larger data storage. These demands will offset the increased component and software efficiency for the foreseeable future. Within the foreseeable future there is little hope that the aggregate kilowatts needed to support classroom computers will decrease significantly.

Power Quality

Each new generation of electronics is faster than its predecessor but also more sensitive to power disturbances. Unlike electric motors and lightbulbs, the solid-state chips in these devices are very sensitive to any kind of perturbation in the power supplied to them. Power irregularities result in erratic performance, processing errors, lost data, and outright equipment damage. The identifiable costs of equipment repairs and data recovery are usually overshadowed by such unmeasured user costs as idle time, repeated work, and frustration. To make matters worse, each year the situation will become a bit more severe. Our dependence on machines grows, and because of their increasing sensitivity to routine power irregularities, the machines are more prone to failure.

The electric utility companies strive to provide customers with power meeting regulatory agency specifications that, in fact, were established before the advent of solid-state electronics. Sometimes, acts of either nature or man intervene, and the power delivered to the building fails to meet standards. Further, electrical variations also can be introduced by electrical equipment within the building; air conditioners, copiers, compressors, and industrial shop equipment are frequent culprits. Therefore, the school itself must assume responsibility for providing "clean" electric power—power purged of the dozens of "routine" irregularities[10,11]—to its computer and communications equipment.

Some elements of the school's electronics require not only a high level of power quality but, because of their pivotal role, a source of power that will not fail. In the event of power failure, computer equipment, such as file servers, require an alternative source of power for enough time to enable an orderly equipment shutdown without risk of data loss. Other equipment, such as the telephone and alarm systems, require power continuity throughout even a protracted emergency. Both types of needs must be satisfied.

Power protection systems are an important element in every school's technical infrastructure, and their selection requires care. The choices can be bewildering. Many kinds of power protection equipment are available. Each has unique performance and economic characteristics, and each must be evaluated on a situation-by-situation basis. Worse yet, terminology differences in product literature make comparisons difficult. (Appendix A gives a more thorough discussion of power quality and power protection equipment.)

If the school's technical staff does not have expertise in power systems for electronics, a consultant should be retained to develop recommendations and possibly assist with the procurement process. Beware of consultants who also sell products.

In addition to power protection equipment, a high-quality earth ground for the building is essential. An effective ground path not only protects personnel and equipment but also provides functions critical to the operation of electronic equipment. For the proper functioning of both electronic and power protection equipment, it is essential.

Static Electricity and Magnetic Fields

As noted previously, computers are sensitive to their electrical environment; the most frequent source of electrical problems is the power delivered to the wall outlet. However, there is another source of electrical problems: static electricity. Often the culprit is synthetic fiber carpeting, especially in winter when the relative humidity in buildings drops below 30%.

Although small computers and peripherals are usually housed in nonconductive plastic cases, it is still possible for users to touch metal conductors, especially when changing cables. If the person happens to become electrically charged, a spark will be drawn between the person and the equipment. These instances can have unpleasant effects ranging from computer software failures to altered data or damaged equipment. It is sensible, therefore, to have nonstatic flooring in computer areas, especially in central equipment rooms and wiring closets. Standard asphalt and vinyl floor tiles meet this requirement, and nonstatic carpeting is available. Where conventional carpeting already is installed, antistatic sprays can be applied routinely. When static problems persist, steps to raise the humidity should be undertaken.

Another overlooked source of problems arises when magnetically encoded media such as floppy disks, magnetic tapes, and even hard disk drives come close to a magnetic field. In these instances, the data can be erased accidentally. The remedy is simple: Educate people to keep magnetic media away from magnets. Magnets are so often used they are unnoticed. Floppy disks have been erased by the magnetic catch on a woman's purse, the bell in a telephone, a refrigerator door message holder, and a loud speaker. Fortunately, magnetic fields diminish with the square of the distance; for example, the field strength at 10 inches is 1/25 the strength at 2 inches. Also, the magnet's effect on the media is not cumulative; repetitive exposures to a weak magnetic field will have no more effect than the first exposure.

Heating, Ventilation, and Air-Conditioning (HVAC)

As mentioned earlier, virtually all of the electrical energy consumed by electronic equipment is converted into heat energy and dissipated into the surrounding space. A monitor plus a fully equipped PC could generate as much as 2,000 BTU (British thermal units) per hour; however, the heat output will rarely be this much because few machines will be configured with the maximum memory and add-on boards. To put this in context: A seated person generates about 200 BTU per hour. The addition of one desktop computer in an office will have only a small effect on the ambient temperature, but when 25 machines and several printers are in a classroom, the heat load becomes substantial. If the actual heat output of each computer is 1,400 BTU per hour, the total additional heat load is more than 36,000 BTU per hour. To remove this heat requires an additional three tons of air-conditioning.[12]

Because there also will be times when the equipment is inoperative, the HVAC requirements can vary from room to room and hour to hour. Not only must the HVAC system be appropriately sized but also the temperature must be controllable at the individual classroom level.

The need for flexibility in the HVAC delivery system extends beyond the capabilities of the thermostat. As the equipment compliment in a room changes over time, the different demand for heating or cooling may even require duct work modifications. For reasons of both flexibility and cost, consideration should be given to an HVAC delivery system located between the subfloor and the working floor where the ducting can be maintained easily. An additional argument for under-the-floor air delivery is reduced heating and cooling costs by the more efficient distribution of make-up air (fresh, outside air brought into the HVAC system to lower the classroom's carbon dioxide level and keep students alert).[13]

Older school buildings often have neither cooling capacity, duct work, nor temperature control systems to meet the needs of rooms with many machines. In these circumstances, when maintaining rooms at desirable temperatures becomes a problem, through-the-wall and window air-conditioning units in each room may be the most effective means to supplement the existing HVAC system. In evaluating either of these options, consideration should be given to the noise level of the units.

Although classroom equipment may be shut down at the close of the day, servers, hubs, and other equipment are always operative and often situated in closed spaces. These wiring closets and equipment rooms with electronic equipment also must be air-conditioned. If the building's air-conditioning system is shut down at night or on weekends, these rooms must have either backup or independent air-conditioning systems. In either case, if the room temperature exceeds some preestablished temperature threshold, there must be means to shut down the electronic equipment automatically before damage is done.

Network

Overview

In the past few years the explosion of the Internet, fueled by the availability of user-friendly software, has amply illustrated Metcalf's Law. Dr. Robert Metcalf, the inventor of the Ethernet, often has stated that the cost of a network increases in proportion to the number of nodes, and the value of the network increases with the square of the number of nodes.

Moreover, the network makes it possible for computing resources to be located where they will be most effective. The large mainframe/dumb terminal architecture locates all the resources on the central computer. The stand-alone PC has all its own resources and access to nothing else. The local area network provides both an opportunity to optimize hardware and software within the school and to rebalance easily as conditions change. Wide-area networks and the Internet dramatically extend the resources that can be at the user's fingertips. The short history of computing can be characterized in three phases: large central host-centric, desktop PC-centric, and now network-centric, where resources are delivered to users as they need them.

Maintainability

The network is a combination of wires, equipment, and software that interconnects all the electronic equipment in the school. It also bridges to networks in other places. In the same way the telephone network connects its customers in a myriad of combinations, the computer network connects individuals to other people and information resources in remote places. Ideally, this connection is completely unnoticed by the user, and the distant services appear to be an integral part of the user's own computer.

The most fundamental criteria for a network are reliability and transparency. These are exemplified by the public telephone system, against which computer networks appear poor by comparison for three reasons. First, the equipment and software for computer networks are in their infancy in relation to the telephone industry. Second, the telephone system is managed by technicians who are hidden from the view of users, whereas all the problems of the school's network must be resolved by the school's people. Finally, minor glitches that are unnoticed in voice communications are a major problem in data communications in which a few lost data bits mean a garbled message.

The network is the glue holding all the sundry pieces of technology together, and Metcalf's thesis is that larger, more encompassing networks are better. Yet the network (hardware, software, and people) is the weakest link and will remain so for the foreseeable future. Recognizing its inherent fragility is the first step in addressing the problem. The second is to heed the five cardinal rules for network success.

1. Design the network to minimize the consequences of network failures.
2. Design the network for ease in determining what has failed and for ease of repair.
3. Install an easily operated network management system that can view the entire network as well as every element in it.
4. Install a competent network administrator and an equally competent backup person.
5. Pursue an active program to train, coach, and support all network users.

Capacity

Bandwidth is the capacity of the network to carry information. The bandwidth of the network is analogous to the capacity of a water pipe; however, instead of gallons per minute, the measure is thousands or millions of bits per second. Technical literature and even newspaper advertisements designate bandwidth in terms of Kbps, meaning kilo (thousand) bits per second, and Mbps for mega (million) bits per second. (Note, when the "b" is capitalized, as in KB, it refers to a byte; by convention, a byte is a group of eight bits.)

Every electronic classroom device needs to be connected to the network, and because classroom needs inevitably change, there must be flexibility in the location of these connection points. Classroom computers can be connected to the local network in many ways, either by a physical connection to a wire or cable, by radio communication, or by infrared transmission. The principal advantages of radio and infrared are the absence of physical connections and their great flexibility within the classroom. The principal advantage of copper wires, coaxial cable, and especially fiber-optic cable is high bandwidth.

Until recently, coaxial cable has been the local area network medium of choice in which high bandwidth was required. Since then, unshielded twisted-pair (similar to telephone wire) technology has improved and is now more cost-effective than coaxial cable in many situations. Now, however, fiber-optic cable technology is used increasingly in high bandwidth situations. At this time, fiber-optic installations are about 30% to 50% more expensive than twisted pair, but this gap is closing. Where fiber-optic cable has been installed, the cost premium has been rationalized by ease of installation, lower maintenance costs, and long-term growth capacity (Telecommunications Industry Association, 1994). The pivotal element in the choice of transmission technology is one's estimate of the future need for bandwidth. The present network traffic is almost completely data: numbers and words. Were network traffic to remain as it is now, it is possible to conceive of a connectionless network within a classroom.[14] Most educators believe, however, that future classroom computing will involve multimedia (sound and full-motion color video) on student monitors. The potential difference in bandwidth required is huge:

- Data to fill one high-resolution monochrome display with text and graphics for 1 minute are approximately 75,000 bytes of information.[15]

- One minute of high-quality color video in a four-inch by three-inch window on the display has more than 300 million bytes of information—4,000 times more data.[16] For some classroom purposes, 15 frames per second and low-quality (8-bit) color will be suitable, and this will reduce the data by more than 80%. Even considering the effectiveness of video compression techniques,[17] modest multimedia applications will increase the bandwidth required in a classroom by a factor of 100 or more.

Multimedia usage will increase network usage significantly; almost certainly this traffic will be beyond the limits of radio and infrared networks. Also, there is a perverse natural law that inexorably increases traffic on a network up to its capacity, much as it does vehicle traffic on a highway. In light of the forces driving increased network use, two recommendations seem evident. Schools must anticipate the need for a physical connection to the network at every location where a computer or other networked device could be placed. (A good rule of thumb is to place a network connection at every potential desk location.) Second, when installed, the network should have the greatest bandwidth affordable.

Of all the various elements of a network, the transmission media has the highest labor cost to install and the lowest component cost. These factors rationalize this advice: When wire and cable are to be installed, use materials capable of supporting the bandwidth envisioned for many years into the future. The overall expense difference will be negligible, especially in comparison to the expense of replacing it. By the same token, when a building is under construction, installation of the building-level network (backbone) wiring should be undertaken even if usage is not anticipated for some years; once the building is completed, installation is hardly trivial.

Design

The probability of high levels of network traffic driven by multimedia applications argues for an architecture minimizing the network load; keep the source of the data as close to the user as possible.

The overall design of the network in a school building should be conceived in three layers: an individual machine layer, a classroom layer, and a building layer. The individual machines should have sufficient memory, hard disk, and CD-ROM to confine most of the data accesses to the machine. At the classroom level, all of the equipment in a single room or, perhaps, even several smaller rooms should be connected to a network dedicated to those machines. Then, a building-level network should interconnect all of the subnetworks in the school complex. This layered configuration keeps intraclassroom traffic off the building-level network. Equally important, it increases overall network reliability because problems are easier to locate, and the effects of most network problems are isolated to one or to a few rooms.

Given this target configuration, the migration from the present state to the final state is straightforward. As classrooms and computer labs are brought on-line, a network is established in each room. When the demand arises for communication between rooms or with other facilities, such as the central file servers or the media center, the building-level network is established. Because the objective is schoolwide connectivity, it is desirable, if not essential, to standardize on a single network technology from the outset. (In a 1992 poll of information systems managers, it was discovered that large companies experienced three times the network downtime as did medium-size companies. It is conjectured that the complexity of the networks in large companies caused the higher failure rate [Hausman, 1994]). At least part of the solution is to constrain the variety of hardware and software products on the network as well as to prohibit products that are likely to cause problems.

Once the building network is established, any classroom modems are removed. All access to services outside the building will be through a communications server on the building-level network. This will not only improve the service level and security but also reduce cost.

Over time, a school district will make substantial investments in the network for equipment, software, and training. Yet regardless of the technology selected, soon much of this investment will be obsolete and slated for change. With thoughtful network design and careful component selection, the inevitable transition to newer technologies can be a series of small increments added to the installed base rather than a wholesale replacement. A primary test of good network design is the ease with which it incorporates future changes.

Technological cul-de-sacs are a frequent hazard. The prudent designer will specify components adhering to broadly accepted industry standards. Although hardware and software that do not adhere to widely accepted standards may not be avoided completely, these products do entail a risk of orphanhood. The product could become isolated from the mainstream of technology development, or the vendor may drop the product line or even go out of business. In respect to the latter possibility, no significant commitment to a vendor should be made without a thorough review of its financial stability. For publicly traded corporations, their annual 10K report (a Securities and Exchange Commission reporting requirement) is the best single source of information. Companies lacking financial stability should never be the source of nonstandard products.

Structured cabling systems are an integrated set of communications cabling and interconnection devices for voice, data, video, and building-control traffic within a building or campus. They comprise standardized, modular components fitting into a star topology and use both unshielded twisted-pair wiring and fiber-optic cable. They can carry voice, data, and video transmissions or a mixture of all of these. These attributes, plus their high capacity and an open-ended design, make them particularly well suited to school systems. Certainly, new construction should specify structured cabling. Appendix F explains more about structured wiring standards.

Figure 2.13 illustrates a school network system that connects all the equipment in a single classroom to a classroom network that is tied to a building-level network. Key aspects of the illustration include the following:

- There is a central equipment room for file servers, communications equipment, and network management facilities. The main power transformer and control equipment are in a separate room.

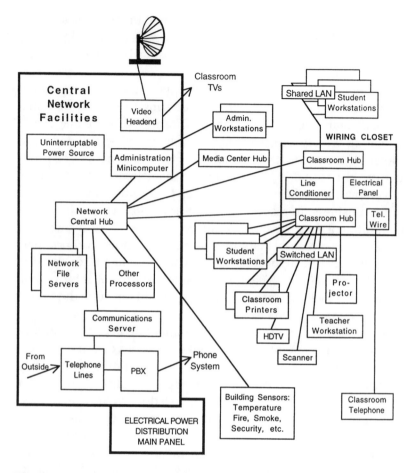

Figure 2.13. Typical Network Topology (not necessarily cable paths)

- The network is used to bring all the building's sensor data, such as smoke and intrusion alarms, into the central control point.
- The centralized equipment is protected by an uninterruptable power system that, in the event of a power failure, enables servers to shut down without damage and maintains power to the telephone equipment and other safety-related equipment.

- Video headend equipment is housed in the central equipment room both for ease of maintenance and to facilitate the future use of the network to deliver the TV signal throughout the school.

- Large host processors and minicomputers also are located in the central equipment room.

- The wiring closet is the transition point between the back-bone wiring that connects to the central network facility and horizontal wiring that distributes signals to the classrooms. It houses the network hub that serves classroom equipment, the telephone wiring panel, a line conditioner that protects computer equipment from power problems (but does not provide uninterruptable service), and an electrical circuit breaker panel. Note that the network and telephone wiring should be kept three feet from the electric circuit breaker panel and the line conditioner. (Similarly, power and copper communications wiring should be in separate conduits.)

At this stage of technology, the best option is to link the classrooms to the central hub with fiber-optic cable.[18] Within the classroom, the computers are tied to the classroom hub with either category 5 (high bandwidth) twisted-pair wiring or fiber-optic cable. At this time, category 5 unshielded twisted-pair wiring in the classroom has a lower first cost than the fiber-optic option, but fiber-optic cable promises less maintenance and greater capacity. The cost of fiber cable and connections is dropping; because the cost advantage of copper is decreasing, a present decision to use copper should be reexamined periodically.

Correct installation of premises communications wiring is critical. Properly installed high-grade wire can carry 100 million bits per second; poorly installed, it will perform badly at 10,000 bits per second. The techniques for installing and testing high-capacity copper wires and fiber-optic cable are stringent and not well understood by many contractors. Poorly drafted specifications lead contractors to underbid contracts and do unsatisfactory work. Schools contracting for the installation of premises communications wiring should use care in drafting a contract that provides for on-site installation inspections, acceptance testing with certified reports of test results, and warranties for both the active and passive elements of the system. Appendix G is a model specification for telecommunications wiring.

The last caveat: Although networks and structured cabling systems are simple in concept, their design is not. Like automobile highways, badly conceived data highways tend to be both ineffective and difficult to rectify. The use of a consultant experienced in the design of local area networks, and another experienced in structured cabling systems, is recommended. These consultants should be brought onboard early in the project; in new construction and major renovation projects, the network consulting contracts should be let when the architecture contract is let. In all instances, consultants should be retained before any equipment and software decisions are made.

Network Wiring Closets

The presence of a network that links together classroom computers, print servers, file servers, and other devices greatly enhances the usefulness of the school's investment in technical resources. The network, however, also adds to the technical environment another layer of complex hardware and software that, when it fails, can hamstring the entire school. Although success in keeping the network operational certainly depends on the skills of the technical staff, it equally depends on how the network equipment is set up and on the diagnostic aids provided.

A key building block of the network is the network hub[19] that ties the classroom machines together and links them to the school network. These hubs should be located in a communications wiring closet (see Figure 2.14). Network maintenance will be made easier if classroom hubs, power protection for the hubs, and the telecommunications patch panel are located in a wiring closet close to the classrooms served. It is ideal if the wiring closet also can house the electrical circuit breaker panel and, if used, the line conditioner protecting the classroom equipment. In this, combined closet care must be taken to keep unshielded network and telecommunications wiring three feet from the power panel and line conditioner. Also, unshielded communications wiring should

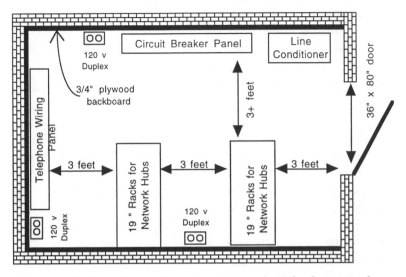

Figure 2.14. Combined Closet for Network, Telephone, and Power

be kept six inches from 120 volt/20 amp circuits that are not in a metal conduit; higher amperages or voltages require still greater separation (American National Standards Institute, 1990).

The size of the closet is a function of the number of computers and telephones to be supported. The American National Standards Institute (1990) suggests 110 square feet of closet to serve 100 workstations, but this does not include space for the circuit breaker panel and line conditioner.

There should be at least one wiring closet per floor or wing, and the wire length from closet to workstation should not exceed 300 feet (American National Standards Institute, 1990).

Because the communications closet has electronics in a confined space, provision must be made to keep the temperature and humidity within limits recommended by the equipment manufacturers.[20] In addition, there should be a thermal switch that will turn off all electronic equipment if the temperature exceeds equipment specifications.

Technical Staff Workspaces

The network support staff requires workspace adjacent to the building's central network equipment. Provision must be made for office space, test equipment, supplies, and parts storage. In large schools or campus arrangements, the technical staff may specialize—some managing the centralized network equipment and others supporting users. When staff members are dedicated to user support, it is desirable to locate their office space near those supported.

To facilitate troubleshooting and routine maintenance, all of the following items should be in a centralized, single location:

- Building-level network hub
- Spare parts
- Building telephone switch
- Diagnostic equipment
- Uninterruptable power source
- File servers
- Communications server
- As-built wiring diagrams, modems, and hardware and software documentation

Support Tools

Not only should the building and the installed equipment be organized for ease of maintenance, but support tools—record-keeping systems, diagnostic equipment, and software that will help manage and maintain the network—also must be provided. Although some of these tools are expensive, they will more than pay for themselves if they enable the school's staff to resolve problems otherwise entailing outside technical assistance. (Outside technicians can be a substantial out-of-pocket cost. Charges of $100 and more per problem resolved over the telephone are not unusual, and on-site technical assistance costs even more.)

In large measure, the robustness of the network is determined by the effectiveness and availability of network support tools. If it cannot be well managed, do not install it.

Notes

1. The New Jersey Institute of Technology (NJIT)—School of Architecture, in cooperation with Apple Computer, has done considerable research on the physical settings for technology-rich learning environments. Its research was based on hundreds of hours of observations and interviews from 1988 to 1992. Two documents from NJIT include Stuebing, Giddings, and Cousineau (1992) and Stuebing, Martin, Wolfshorndl, and Cousineau (1992). Another source document is Apple Computer (1991).

2. Rea's (1991) article is an excellent review of the subject and offers specific suggestions to address glare and reflections.

3. If a mesh-type antiglare screen is to be used, it should be certified by the manufacturer as appropriate for that display. An inappropriate mesh can produce a moiré (interference pattern) and other undesirable side effects.

4. The American Academy of Ophthalmology states that based on scientific evidence, VDTs pose no hazard to the eyes.

5. Users with expert-level keyboard skills may prefer that the display be placed at the customary, slightly-below-horizontal position; however, those who frequently look at the keyboard usually find a display positioned 20 to 40 degrees below the horizontal less tiring.

6. The Swedish Confederation of Professional Employees (TCO) has actively promoted safety for office workers. In 1992, the organization determined that the MPR II standard did not offer sufficient protection; as a result, the TCO'92 standard was created. TCO recently has announced TCO'95, which sets standards for screen flicker, linearity, luminance, and brilliance; in addition, it also establishes a number of standards for keyboards.

7. ANSI/EIA/TIA Standard 569 for commercial building wiring recommends that troughs be spaced five to six feet apart in office

areas, but this is on the assumption that there will be only one workstation per 100 square feet.

8. The additional power required to remove the heat generated by the electronics is approximately half of the power consumed by the electronics.

9. These power requirements are taken from equipment nameplates. Note, however, that nameplate values are based on equipment with the maximum configuration and so probably overstate the power required for typical equipment.

	Amps @120 volts
Apple Power Macintosh® 6100/60	3
Apple audiovisual color monitor	1.3
Sony 15" color monitor	1
Canon PC w/90Mhz microprocessor	4
Hewlett Packard Laserjet 4 Plus® printer 12 pg./min. (printing mode)	5.5

10. Goldstein and Speranza's (1982) report documents an average of 53 power disturbances per year.

11. Allen and Segall's (1974) report documents an average of 44 power disturbances per year.

12. 12,000 BTU = 1 ton of cooling capacity. If heat output is calculated solely on the basis of nameplate data, air-conditioning units may be oversized, and oversized units do not dehumidify well. Heat load estimates should be based on actual power consumption measurements.

13. Milam's (1992) study concludes that an underfloor air distribution system has both lower installation and operating costs. Lower HVAC and electrical maintenance costs were not used in the calculation.

14. Where radio frequency communications are contemplated within the classroom or school building, the need for RF shielding level should be investigated.

15. A typical 14-inch monochrome display is made up of 640 by 480 pixels (picture elements; i.e., dots) or a total of 307,000 bits (38,000 bytes) of information. If two different images are needed

to support a user for a minute, the total data required is 76,000 bytes.

16. At 72 pixels per inch, there are 62,208 pixels in the 4-inch by 3-inch area. If 24-bit color is used, then about 1.5 million bits are needed to describe a single image. At 30 images per second for a 60-second period, the total data required is approximately 336 million bytes. (Note that television uses 30 frames per second and motion pictures, 24).

17. Image compression techniques reduce the file size of computer images by identifying and eliminating nonessential information. One recently developed image compression technique (HARC-C) can reduce the data storage required for a single frame of color video by 10:1 or more with little or no visible loss of image quality. Even greater reduction is possible if additional processing is possible or some image degradation is acceptable.

18. Because each building on a campus is separately grounded, all communications cables between the buildings should be fiber-optic to avoid damaging "ground loops."

19. A *hub* in this book is a generic device. It functions both to switch traffic among workstations within the classroom and to route traffic to other network equipment within the school. It also may be a bridge between one network protocol and another.

20. A case in point is that uninterruptable power supply batteries will last only half as long at 87° F as they will at 77° F.

CHAPTER 3

Ensuring Physical and Data Security

SYNOPSIS

 As computers become more integrated into daily activities and more information is committed to electronic storage, the issues of physical and data security come to the forefront.

Physical security is the protection of the equipment from fire, vandalism, or theft. In addition to the usual measures of locks, smoke detectors, and sprinkler systems, schools should take steps to control access to equipment rooms and wiring closets and install devices to protect electronics from high temperatures. Also, a record of all equipment and software serial numbers should be maintained and an annual inventory taken.

Data security is the protection of data from loss, corruption, or unauthorized access. Protection of data is critical to the school's operations:

- Lost data will be time-consuming and difficult to re-create, and data without a hard copy source may be impossible to restore.

- Unauthorized access to personnel and other confidential files has legal risks.
- Unauthorized copying of licensed software exposes the school to both civil and criminal penalties.
- Computer viruses can both destroy data and disable computers.

The only sure protection from accidental loss of data is redundancy—current copies of the data with one copy being kept outside the school building.

Control of unauthorized access to data is a formidable problem because it is difficult to detect and prevent. Worse yet, once machines are attached to a network and access from the outside world is possible, schools become a target for hackers worldwide. There is a plethora of access protection methods ranging from simple password systems to firewalls and encryption schemes that are indecipherable by the CIA. All have their cost, and school boards should take these steps:

- Evaluate their various security needs.
- Install security mechanisms appropriate to each need.
- Recognize that many breaches are papers in a wastebasket or a password taped to the desk and implement an ongoing security awareness program for all employees.

Finally, all physical and data protection programs can fail. School superintendents should insist on both a written contingency plan and an annual testing of the plan.

Background

Computer technology in schools gives rise to new security concerns. As the technology infiltrates the school's classrooms and offices, many if not most of the school's activities gradually will become dependent on the technology. The school then becomes vulnerable to anything that disrupts the machines or the network interconnecting them. Indeed, when the technology fails, activity ceases. Security, therefore, must become a principal concern of school boards and senior administrators.

Security considerations fall neatly into two classes: (a) the protection of the physical plant from fire, vandalism, or theft and (b) the protection of the data from destruction, corruption, or unauthorized access. Of the two, the physical plant is easier to protect from hazards than the data. Locked doors, fences, and closed-circuit security videocameras are effective deterrents to vandals and burglars. Data security breaches are less tangible, less detectable, and potentially much more serious than breakdowns in physical security. Also, once a network cable or phone line is connected to a machine, the risk to data escalates.

Plant Security

In addition to the usual school physical security measures such as smoke detectors, fire-resistant doors, and sprinkler systems, the following minimum provisions should be in place:

- Maintain a record of the serial numbers of all hardware and software and take a physical inventory at least once a year.
- Keep the wiring closet locked.
- Limit equipment room access to the network support staff. Card key locks are effective if many technicians need access.
- Verify the identities of all repair personnel and technicians.
- Install an intrusion alarm system in the central equipment room; ideally, the central equipment space should be in a space with neither windows nor doors to the outside of the building.
- Provide an alarm system triggered by temperatures over 90° F to provide a safe margin before electronics are damaged. If the alarm is not answered, the equipment should be turned off automatically.
- Install a switch near the door cutting off power to all equipment.

Data Security

Overview

As used here, the term *data* is all-inclusive and refers to all the information resident in any of the equipment or passing over the network. Data files include official school records, staff and teacher correspondence and private documents, student files, libraries of instructional materials, and software. Data are a huge investment and their protection is critical to the operation of the school system:

- Some of the data in electronic form have no hard copy counterpart—if the data are lost, they cannot be re-created. For example, attendance data may be entered directly into the computer by the teacher; if the data are subsequently lost, no source documents exist from which to reenter the data.
- Even when data can be re-created from source documents, reconstruction can be prohibitively expensive and, in any case, difficult and time-consuming.
- Access to personnel and other files by unauthorized persons also has large legal risks.
- Unauthorized copying of licensed software can expose the school to both civil and criminal legal action.[1]

Failure is inevitable for all mechanical, electronic, and software devices. When computers fail, the loss of data is probable unless defensive measures have been taken. Failure of businesses to protect data has put some businesses in bankruptcy and others in court. Negligent school systems can suffer equally serious consequences.

The only sure defense against data loss is redundancy—a current copy of the data maintained on another machine or on a removable medium such as tape or disk. File backups are the single most effective data security measure. Daily, users should back up their workstation files to the central file server and, in turn, the technical support staff must make a copy of the central server files and store them in another building. The best practice is to keep two generations of backup files: the most recent and its predecessor.

Data Access Control

Control of data access can be as simple as keeping the machine under lock and key and disconnected from the network. The network connection makes security inherently more difficult, especially if the network can be accessed through the public telephone system. In an Ernst and Young study of 1,271 companies, 20% of those surveyed reported problems because of people breaking into their computer systems (Sandberg, 1994). In some circles, breaking into networks and perusing or destroying data is considered a competitive sport. Schools must assume that computer hackers and crackers will attempt to breach the security system and, when successful, that they will do serious damage.

Access control has to be approached on two levels. The basic level is to prevent unauthorized persons from gaining use of the network or access to data files. Probably, the most practical means of validating the identity of potential users is a password system. Once the user identity is confirmed, the user is given access to network facilities and authorized data files.[2] If the user does not divulge the password to anyone and obvious passwords such as birth dates are avoided, a password scheme can be an effective security measure. Three good rules for passwords are these:

- Passwords should be at least eight characters long and include one or more nonalphabetic characters.
- Passwords should be changed frequently.
- Unencrypted passwords should not be sent over a network.

The second level of data security is achieved by the use of hardware or software to encrypt the data to be kept private. Here, the level of security is improved significantly because even if the password is compromised, the user also must have the secret key to decrypt the data. If the encryption and decryption functions are done at the workstation instead of at the file server or main frame, then encryption also can prevent the compromise of private data during communications by devices such as telephone taps. Although data encryption and subsequent decryption carry a cost and speed penalty, they do provide a virtual guarantee of privacy.

Another application of encryption to enhance security is the encoding of the password tables in the software. Even when a hacker is able to penetrate the operating system, the list of valid passwords is unintelligible. Password encryption should be included in software purchase specifications whenever there is need for a high level of data security. Some caution is advisable when adopting password encryption; users forgetting their password have a serious problem—their password-protected files are forever inaccessible.

When cryptography is adopted as part of the security system, the quality of the encryption method is important. It has been reported that Crack, an easily available password discovery program, was able find 50 passwords in 10 minutes and 90 in 30 minutes when it was applied to encrypted password files containing 1,594 passwords (Frisch, 1994). There are, however, encryption methods that, to date, have proven to be unbreakable. The DES (Data Encryption Standard), a secret key[3] system, and PGP (Pretty Good Privacy), a public key system, are both widely available in the United States. Unfortunately, some software packages employ encryption algorithms that are far less robust. Before adopting encryption as a central element in its security strategy, a school should carefully assess the strength of the proposed scheme[4] in light of its needs. Also, if the system might be used by foreign nationals or be used in a foreign country, the school should become familiar with current U.S. federal regulations.[5]

When the school's network can be accessed by public telephone lines, an additional level of security may be appropriate to frustrate persons trying to gain unauthorized access. An effective means is a dial-back system that limits remote access to selected phone numbers. When a dial-up connection is made and a proper user name and password entered, the system breaks the phone connection and then dials the telephone number associated with that user.

Another security mechanism is a firewall. Although there are several different types of firewalls, they all interpose specialized electronics and software between the internal and external networks. (Eighty percent of the computer crimes investigated by the FBI involved unauthorized access through the Internet.) A firewall is a gateway that blocks intruders and also unwanted outgoing communications. Although neither physical nor communications firewalls are 100% secure, if well constructed, they can provide a high level of protection.

Where data must be guaranteed secure from electronic intrusion, the best way to protect the data is by using a machine not connected to the network and keeping the data on a removable medium, such as a floppy disk, that is stored in a locked safe when not in use. Equal care must be taken with ostensibly erased floppy disks; if the data have not been overwritten, they can be recovered with readily available software. Also, if printed output is not tightly controlled, concern about electronic intrusion is pointless.

Good access control means users have easy access to data and facilities within the scope of their authorization, but unauthorized access is exceedingly difficult or impossible. Striking a balance between ease of access by authorized users and adequate protection requires careful consideration of the risks involved.

The statistics shown in Figure 3.1 may help put the foregoing discussion into perspective—to quote Pogo, "We have met the enemy and he is us."

The most subtle security problem is the introduction of a virus into the system. A virus is a tiny computer program hidden in a larger program. The virus has two functions: It is to do something, such as corrupt a resident program or data, and to reproduce itself. When program information is passed to another machine, the virus sends along a copy of itself to do the same thing in the next machine. The consequences of a virus in a network can be severe because it can quickly propagate to every device in the system and thus cripple the entire school system. Sometimes a virus has propagated to thousands of machines in a matter of days. Some viruses are benign, but often the damage done to data files by viruses can be expensive, time-consuming, and, in some instances, almost impossible to restore.

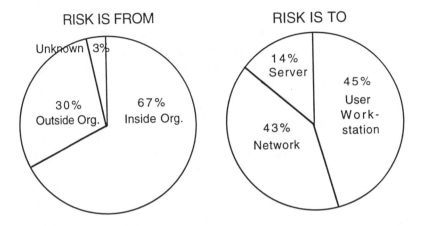

Figure 3.1. Security Risks
NOTE: Most risks begin inside the organization and affect workstations and the network.

Networked machines are uniquely exposed to virus hazards, but even stand-alone machines are vulnerable through the sharing of floppy disks. It is virtually impossible to police every data file and program brought into the school system. Every server and user workstation, therefore, should be shielded by virus protection software. Even with this in place, staff, teachers, and students should be discouraged from introducing data files and programs from "foreign sources" into the school's system. Imported information should be taken only from sources known to be reliable, and, regardless of the source, imports always should be screened by a virus detection program.

Virus detection software is effective only to the extent that it has been programmed to recognize the virus at hand. Virus detection developers provide their customers with updates as they become aware of new viruses. However, because still newer viruses are always floating around, all users should be briefed about the most likely sources of viruses, typical symptoms of viral infection, and what to do if one is suspected.

New ingenious security mechanisms are being introduced constantly; however, security programs that focus only on the technology are misleading. Indeed, often the largest gaps in the security system are papers left on desks or tossed into a wastebasket and unattended machines logged onto the network. The foregoing recommendations notwithstanding, the single most effective data security measure is the education and training of all those in contact with the network. They all must understand the meaning of data security, their own responsibilities, and the consequences of their failures. A password system is of little use if the password is taped to the keyboard. Security must become a habit as much as locking the ignition when leaving the car.

Finally, at best, a security system only can implement the policies of the organization. Investments in security equipment and software must be in direct support of a school policy that clearly establishes what is to be protected and the degree of protection required. If there is no clear policy, defer any significant investment.

Accidental Data Damage

Accidentally erased files and changes inadvertently made to programs can disrupt classroom operations. Mistakes by novice and even more experienced users are a source of problems that can be easily reduced or avoided. A number of products effectively keep the user out of trouble; they limit the user's options to those selected by the teacher or technical staff. One product for the elementary school market displays a street scene cartoon when the machine is turned on. Each storefront is a different application that is accessed by "opening" the store's door; the user's actions are limited to entering the stores on the street or to turning off the machine.

On-Line Bulletin Boards

A natural outgrowth of networked computers are on-line bulletin boards, the electronic equivalent of a conventional bulletin board, where anybody with a thumbtack can post an item to be read by all. The electronic version is similar, in that any person with access to the message board can read or copy any message or post an original message. The principal difference is that the electronic messages can be more than simple text messages; they can be anything in digital form, including pictures, music, computer programs, and large data files.

Many school networks have on-line bulletin boards because they are useful. However, schools that have electronic bulletin boards should also impose standards for their use.

Bulletin board services are proliferating at an astounding pace, and until recently there have been no court decisions regarding the liability of the operators of these on-line services. Now, however, cases are appearing in state and federal courts. One recent case in Florida (*Playboy Enterprises v. Frena*, 1993) involved the operator of a bulletin board. Without the approval of the operator, a subscriber posted copies of pictures from *Playboy* magazine. The court held that the operator's lack of knowledge was no excuse and he was found guilty of copyright infringement. *Stratton Oakmont, Inc. and Daniel Poruse v. Prodigy Services Co. et al.* (1994) was a similar case. The New York Supreme Court found that Prodigy could be held accountable for the content of on-line messages because Prodigy exercised editorial control by screening material for obscenities. In light of court rulings, the dilemma of schools is whether to exercise control over network postings at some legal risk or exercise no control and risk the consequences of public outcry.

Contingency Planning

It is not a question of whether a disaster will happen but what the consequences will be when one does happen. As more and more data are committed to electronic storage and as the daily operations of both classrooms and administration offices come to depend on the computer, it is necessary to consider contingency planning.

The chart in Figure 3.2 classifies the common disasters affecting computers. Note that no sure way of preventing any of them is known.

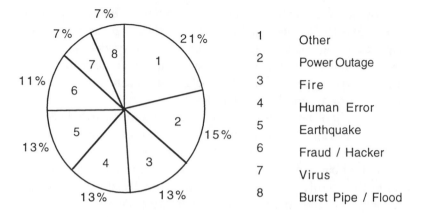

Figure 3.2. Common Computer Disasters

Contingency planning is an integral aspect of any well-managed school system. All schools have periodic fire drills and perhaps tornado or other drills, because this modicum of planning and practice may have a high payoff in the future. By the same token, it is necessary to consider events that could disable or destroy the school's technical environment. Property and liability insurance are essential, but they are not a substitute for thoughtful planning. In planning for contingencies the two core questions are these:

- When an unfortunate occurrence does happen, to what extent will it impair the operations of the school?
- What affordable steps are available to make the consequences less severe?

The process of contingency planning begins with an inventory of all hardware and software and a documented network topology. Then, element by element, the consequences of loss are considered and plans made for actions to be taken now or in the future to minimize the effect of a failure. For instance, if state aid is based on student days and all the attendance records are maintained in a computer database, what happens if the database is destroyed and what steps should be taken now to preclude irrevocable losses? If academic records are destroyed, how can they be restored?

Often, the actions are simple and low cost. Faithfully followed file backup procedures are certainly a key element for the preservation of data in any contingency plan.

A contingency plan, however, also must address other possible happenings that could disrupt or disable a school. One organization with a sprinkler system in the central server room raised the equipment off the floor and kept plastic covers over inoperative equipment. Another identified other equipment that could be reallocated to certain critical tasks. In industry, it is not unusual for one company to have arrangements with another to share computer resources on an emergency basis. Also, some companies are in the business of providing standby computing capabilities to those without sufficient justification of having their own.

As with any plan, a contingency plan is useful only if it is workable, current, and understood by all. At least annually, the plan must be taken off the shelf and updated with all recent technical and organizational changes. Moreover, the plan should be reviewed by key faculty and administrators to validate the implicit priorities. As with fire drills, there must be carefully scripted, simulated disasters to test both the concepts of the contingency plan and the training of the personnel. Postmortems after the tests will reveal much about the validity of the plan and the level of security it actually provides.

Notes

1. The Copyright Act in Title 17 of the U.S. Code applies to software and provides for as much as $100,000 in statutory damages per copyright violation. It also provides for criminal penalties of as much as $250,000 and jail terms of up to 5 years in addition to civil penalties.

2. Many software packages permit still further discrimination. They enable security administrators to specify for each database, or even each data element, the types of privileges granted to each

person. For instance, one person may be authorized only to read the data, whereas another also may be able to modify the data.

3. Appendix H is a description of secret and public key cryptographic systems.

4. In any encryption scheme, the level of security is proportional to the square of the key size. At present, a 40-bit key will provide reasonable security, and a 64-bit key has yet to be broken. Note, however, that as the power of computers increases, the key must be larger to maintain equivalent security.

5. Many cryptographic systems are classified as munitions by the U.S. Department of State. Use of these by certain foreign nationals, and use in foreign countries, is restricted. The Office of Defense Trade Controls, Bureau of Political-Military Affairs, U.S. State Department will provide copies of the current regulations on request.

CHAPTER 4

Adopting
Appropriate Policies

SYNOPSIS

School policies should not only change to reflect the opportunities and risks of the information age but also change before a crisis rather than in the midst of it. Appendix D includes a set of 29 policies that can be adapted easily to the needs of a school system. The rationale behind most of them is self-evident. A few policy subjects, however, benefit from some explanation.

Islands of Technology. When organizations are allowed to select technology without constraint, islands of technology develop that prevent or inhibit communications beyond their own boundaries. Because most of the benefits of computer technology result from data communications, these islands diminish the benefits to the entire school system. Moreover, once installed, nonstandard technology becomes a virtually permanent fixture draining technical staff resources. The solution is a well-thought-out technical architecture backed by management resolve to make it stick.

Privacy. A locked file cabinet no longer ensures the information privacy necessary for the operation of a school. Computers, especially when networked, introduce new vulnerabilities, some with severe consequences. The basic privacy concepts are these:

- Access is granted only to those who need access.
- The sensitivity of the data determines the security level.
- The "owner" of the data (usually the author of the data) is responsible for determining who may access the data and for setting the proper security level.

Every school system has information that, if copied or disclosed, would open the school to legal action. There are no sure means to prevent this, and the school board's best defense is to have (a) written policies regarding privacy of information and the unauthorized copying of copyrighted material and (b) proof that the policies are enforced systematically.

Ownership of Employee Creations. It is quite possible that a school employee or contractor will develop unique software or hardware that has commercial value. It is important to establish ownership of these creations before the creation is sold—a school board claiming title after the fact will result in a bitter dispute or even a lawsuit. In industry, employment contracts routinely specify that all intellectual creations belong to the company. School policy should be established and appended to employment contracts.

Inappropriate Information. Once classroom computers can access information outside of the school's domain, it is possible that employees or students will be exposed to data and images that they (or the parents of students) will find offensive. The network is analogous to a public library where, if a book is offensive, the patron should not read it. Although there is software designed to block unwanted data sources, there is no assurance that it will filter out all offensive material. School administrators should forewarn employees, students, and parents of students of the risk of exposure to offensive material and absolve the school of responsibility for either controlling students or blocking out all that is offensive.

Network Safety. School networks provide their employees and students an opportunity to interact with strangers. As in other meetings with strangers, certain precautions should be taken. For example, unencrypted credit card numbers should not be transmitted; neither should names, addresses, and phone numbers be "posted" in public forums. Similarly, students should not meet network friends without adult supervision.

Media Center. Within a school there needs to be a focal point for the management of computer-based instructional material. A media center is recommended.

Vendor Dispute Resolution. Disputes sometimes arise in transactions involving complex technology. It is recommended that contracts contain a binding arbitration clause; sample clauses are in Appendix E. In the event that disputes are not resolved amicably, they will be resolved before a panel of experts rather than by a judge or jury who probably has little understanding of the technology. The proceedings will be less formal, less costly, and move with less delay.

Background

Scientist and author C. P. Snow observed, "Technology is a queer thing. . . . It brings great gifts with one hand, and it stabs you in the back with the other" (*Webster's New Riverside Desk Quotations,* 1992, p. 158).

The widespread use of computers in society is a relatively new phenomenon, but these machines are changing the fabric of our culture rapidly.[1] In some cases, such as illegal software copying, the necessary policies are plainly evident. In other cases, the issue is evident but the resolution is not; for example, to what lengths must database "owners" go to ensure the correctness of the data, and what is their liability for incorrect data? Many of the needed policies, such as intellectual property rights and privacy, are already in existence, but they must now be tuned to the peculiarities of the computer era. We will never have complete foresight, but we should recognize potential problems and try to address them at the outset; later on, it can be an uphill struggle or even a lost cause.

The ramifications of the new technologies are seen in every cranny. As in the previous chapter, this chapter will address a wide range of topics linked by the common thread of information technology. In most school systems, the responsibility for each of these related elements often is scattered across the organization chart, with no single point of responsibility and accountability for the overall technical environment. The challenge for senior school officials is to overlook the boundaries of organizational turf and holistically address the implications of the new technologies in all their varied aspects.

Control of information access and presentation confers power; the politics of information technology are inevitably the politics of power. Only the school superintendent or the school board is in a position to resolve the politics of information technology—for example, who decides technical issues, who controls the technology budget, and who makes the call on how technology is applied in the classroom or in the office. Without crisp policies, the intramural wars and negotiated settlements will lead to a chaos of incompatible bits of technology. Appendix D is a model set of policies; they can be adapted to any school system easily. This chapter explores those policies in which the underlying rationale may not be self-evident:

Islands of technology
Privacy
Ownership of hardware and software developed by employees
Inappropriate information
Network safety
Media center/library
Vendor dispute resolution

Discussion

Islands of Technology

If organizational units, such as the English Department or the fourth grade, are allowed to select technology without constraints, isolated islands of technology will develop that cannot communicate with other areas of the school. Although they possibly may be the best solutions for that particular group, they may be less than optimal for the entire school system. Much of the benefit of computer and telecommunications technology is the sharing of information among its users. If these islands are allowed to develop or persist, this benefit is diminished or lost entirely.

The solution to this dilemma is to adopt and enforce a set of technical standards promoting a graceful interchange of information among groups and, at the same time, give the organizational units considerable license within the constraints imposed by the standards. The following recommended standards address those aspects of equipment, data transmission, and applications software that are most essential to the flow of information and the minimization of technical support costs. (As will be discussed later, there is an incentive to constrain the permitted options: The large suites of hardware and software have greater support costs.)

Equipment Standards

- Microprocessor family (e.g., Intel x86, Motorola PowerPC®)
- Interface standard (e.g., VESA, EISA, PCI)
- Minimum amount of memory and disk storage (e.g., 16 mB memory and 300 mB disk storage)
- Operating system (e.g., Windows'95®, Windows NT®, OS2®, UNIX®, Macintosh®)
- Antivirus software

Data Transmission Standards

- Media (e.g., fiber-optic cable, twisted-pair category 5)

- Protocol (e.g., 10 Base T Ethernet, 16 mb Token Ring)
- Network operating system (e.g., Novell Netware®, Banyan Vines®)

Applications Software Standards

- Word processing
- Spreadsheet
- Database
- Electronic mail
- Presentation

Specifically not included is any mention of the PC manufacturer, display size, personal productivity tools, drawing programs, and screen savers; none of these significantly impinge on the flow of information. Also not included are academic applications peculiar to a certain grade level or discipline. Academic software should be selected by those who will use it; however, even here there is an argument for some constraint on complete laissez faire. For example, if the fourth-grade teachers in a school agree on the software they will use, there will be opportunities for the teachers to share ideas and know-how; there also may be possible procurement economies. It is beyond the scope of this book, however, to prescribe academic procedures.

Widely accepted international standards, de facto industry standards, and the direction of mainstream technology all should bear heavily on how the school's technical standards are drafted. Well-chosen standards are the single best insurance for investments that can stand the test of time. Moreover, when developing and introducing standards, special attention also should be given to the needs and sensitivities of the user community. Solicitation of user suggestions, consultation, and feedback must be integral parts of any standards development program. It is natural for people to chafe at constraints and, without grassroots support, even the most obviously beneficial standards will be ignored or evaded.

An artful compromise must be struck that balances the more or less unique needs of each unit against the objectives of overall economy and information interchange. Whatever the balance, standards will be most effective when they are in place and enforced from the outset. Once an organization has made a psychological and financial investment in "nonstandard" hardware or software products, these products, quite literally take on lives of their own; often it takes years for these situations to run their course.

Even when there is already a plethora of incompatible technologies installed, imposing standards is important. The standards will keep the situation from becoming worse and, over time, normal obsolescence and replacement will gradually eliminate the nonstandard elements.

Technical standards also can affect the cost and quality of technical support significantly. One frustrated chief information officer is reputed to have said, "The odd-ball fringe may only be a fringe but it costs me a bloody fortune." Over a period of time, a number of units in the company had introduced software (and some hardware) that were outside of the company's standards. With each new software product, another technical support person plus a backup had to be assigned and trained; even then, information interchange often was stymied. Still worse, technical and political considerations had made these products virtually permanent fixtures.

Privacy

Data privacy is the other side of the previously discussed data security coin. Data security is concerned with preventing unauthorized access, but privacy is concerned with who is authorized to access the data. Can security and privacy be overemphasized? Hardly. Computer and communications technologies have introduced new threats to privacy that cannot be ignored. As noted by Peter Neumann (1994), "Every abuse that is possible without computers can be amplified in place, time and extent [with computers]; furthermore, new abuses become possible" (p. 138).

The idea of privacy is fundamental to U.S. values. Searching a person's home, tapping a telephone, opening mail, and plagiarizing writings all are addressed in our legal and cultural systems. Now, however, computers and communications technologies are bringing new issues into focus, calling for new interpretations of old principles. Many issues are relevant to school systems. For instance, copyrighted electronic material in the media center is a potential source of problems because the "fair use" rules,[2] which were established for copying printed material, have yet to address all the nuances of electronic documents, images, and sound.

If privacy issues were not addressed when computers were first brought into the school system, they assuredly must be addressed when they are networked. As with the U.S. Postal Service or the telephone system, users must trust the technology. They need to know that their private communications and files are secure from all to whom they have not granted access. Without this trust, the systems lose most of their value—few would mail a letter that was to be read by several strangers before delivery or use a telephone system subject to eavesdropping.

At the working level, privacy must be addressed on a case-by-case basis—what rights (read-only, adding, deleting, etc.) are to be granted to each person or group of people for each piece of information. The basic privacy concepts are these:

- Access is granted only to those needing access.
- The consequence of unauthorized access (i.e., sensitivity of the data) determines the level of security surrounding the data.
- The "owner" of the data (usually the creator of the data) is responsible for determining who may access the data and the appropriate level of security. The owner, of course, must be guided by the school's policies on privacy.

Although the school system must provide software tools enabling data privacy measures, most of the responsibility for privacy administration rests with the owners of the data. If information privacy policies are to be more than cosmetic, then everyone must be reminded frequently of their role in maintaining them, and those breaching the policy must not go unscathed.

School boards have a large potential legal exposure. The board can be held liable if an employee improperly uses, copies, or discloses protected material, and, under present law, it may be difficult to avoid the risk of litigation.[3] No sure means exist to prevent an employee or student from improperly using data and exposing the board to legal action. The board's best defense is to have written policies regarding privacy of information and intellectual property rights. In addition, the board must be able to show how these policies are effectively disseminated and vigorously enforced throughout the system.

Employment and consulting contracts should have explicit confidentiality clauses and should clearly establish ownership of any software developed during the term of the contract. The school should have a program to periodically remind employees, contractors, and consultants of their role in data privacy administration and also of their obligations under software licenses and copyright law. Teachers must regularly take these messages to their students. (Appendix B is a discussion of software and copyright law.)

Privacy and, more broadly, the protection of intellectual property rights are ultimately the responsibility of individuals, but the school board and senior administration officials must establish the school's policies and guidelines. Electronic technology is changing rapidly, and the relevant laws are still evolving. Periodically, therefore, the board should require a policy review by both the director of technology and its legal counsel.

Privacy is not absolute, however. Employees have been discharged or have faced legal action after the contents of their electronic mail and electronic files have been read by an employer. Employers have successfully claimed that their equipment has created, stored, or delivered the information, and, therefore, they have the right to peruse employees' files. Although this is not a frequent issue, it is always an incendiary one because employees assume their desk key and their password guarantee them privacy. Whatever it is, the school's policy should be clear and all employees aware of it.

Although not inclusive, the list below is a thought-jogger—a list of possible topics to be addressed in privacy policies and procedures. Each should be considered from these three perspectives:

1. Who needs access to the information?
2. What are the barriers to unauthorized access?
3. What is to be done about breaches of privacy policy?

Administrative Information

- School board: minutes, reports, correspondence
- Financial data: financial records, purchase records, contracts
- Student data: grades, test scores, attendance, medical, and discipline records
- Employee data: personnel files, salary and payroll data, medical data, performance evaluations, correspondence
- School-owned software and library materials in electronic media
- All other administrative data such as official correspondence, school bus schedules, building maintenance records, athletic schedules

Faculty and Staff Information

- Lecture notes, employee-owned teaching aids, lesson plans
- Correspondence, personal notes
- Employee-developed software
- Employee-owned software

Student Information

- Students' completed work and work in-process
- Students' personal records such as class notes
- Student-developed software
- Student-owned software

Ownership of Employee Creations

It is quite possible that a teacher or other employee will develop new software that has commercial appeal. The issue of ownership of intellectual creations by employees and contractors should be resolved before the issue arises. Acrimonious and expensive litigation often has resulted when an employee's creation has been sold by the employee and the employer claims ownership of the invention even though the invention was not part of the employee's work scope. Of course, if the situation is reversed and the employer sells an employee's invention, there is an opportunity equally ripe for dispute.

Corporations often establish their ownership of all intellectual creations of their employees as a condition of employment. These agreements usually include all intellectual creations by the employee regardless of whether the idea or work was done during working hours or on personal time and regardless of its relationship to the employee's assignment. Companies routinely grant employees exceptions when the creation is outside the commercial interests to the company.

Development of new software can be very lucrative, and it particularly lends itself to development by a lone person; only a creative mind and access to a computer are necessary. Schools may be a particularly fertile breeding ground for educational software, and school boards should establish a policy and reference it in their standard employment contract. But because there is no employee or contractual relationship with students, public schools probably have no claim on the inventions of students.

Inappropriate Information

Problems leading to legal action can arise when the resources of the school system are directly or indirectly involved in exposing employees and students to words and images that the recipients or, in the case of students, parents consider offensive. Even in circumstances without legal implications, inappropriate materials can easily distract attention from the mission of educating children.

It is possible for school administrators to control the books and periodicals in the classrooms and on library shelves, markedly reducing the possibility of people encountering offensive material. However, as school networks mature, they will inevitably establish connections with computers in other schools, libraries, universities, and public forums. Once school computers access information beyond the confines of the local school system, the range of information accessible to any user is almost infinite. Undoubtedly, material is there that some will find offensive, and because school computers are involved, some may consider the school accountable for that. When access to outside resources is enabled, no practical means exist to screen out offensive materials or block access to every possible source of such material. The most effective remedies are in the realm of policy.

Two policies should be considered. First, it is the responsibility of school officials to forewarn employees, students, and parents of the possibility of exposure to offensive materials in information sources beyond the school's control, and when the situation does occur, it is the user's responsibility to terminate the session immediately and inform the teacher or supervisor. Some schools require parents to sign a permission form for a student to have access to outside resources; the form acknowledges that the school is not able to censor what their child might find on the network (Flanders, 1994). Second, if such a policy is not already in existence, there should be a policy that no one should knowingly place another in a position in which he or she will be exposed to material that person finds offensive.

Network Safety

When children are very young, they are given strict rules by their parents that are designed to protect them from untoward meetings with strangers. Children, for example, are told not to take candy from strangers or get in their automobile. Computer networks, especially those that provide unsupervised on-line discussions, have similar risks and similar admonitions that are appropriate. The following are several basic guidelines that schools might consider.

- Never publish identifying information—name, address, or phone number—in a public forum such as an electronic bulletin board.

- Provide identifying information in electronic mail only after consulting with a teacher.
- Never put a credit card or bank account number in an unencrypted electronic message and then only do so with established, well-known correspondents.
- Never arrange to meet with a "network acquaintance" without a teacher being present.
- Never respond to any electronic message that is obscene or threatening or makes one feel uncomfortable.

Media Center or Library

The school library, now often called the media center, should be the repository for all educational reference material in electronic media. The media director should control the acquisition of all electronic reference material for the school district, and all the schools' libraries should be networked together. The media center also should be the center of competence for distance learning and educational television broadcasts. In addition, the media specialist must be the resident expert in the vast array of knowledge bases, all of which can be instantly accessed through the network. Although the media center is clearly responsible for the management and administrative aspects of these remote resources, the technical staff must remain responsible for the installation and support of the technology.

As the media center becomes the locus for all electronic educational materials, media directors should review current software licenses for opportunities to reduce costs.[4] For instance, when teaching materials can be stored on a central server instead of on individual classroom machines, it is certainly possible that fewer copies will be needed. With high-speed communications links, it even may be possible to support an entire school district with a single copy of some material on a central server. In addition, from their central position in the procurement process, the media center staff may be able to negotiate better terms from suppliers: lower prices and installation, training, and support concessions.

Centralization of educational software will alter network traffic patterns. It certainly will place more traffic on the network pieces connecting classrooms to the media center; a trend must be closely monitored to anticipate and avoid network saturation. As the role of the media center expands to include electronic media delivered by the network, the director of technology must be part of the planning process.

Vendor Dispute Resolution

Although most business transactions are executed without incident, sometimes disputes arise, especially in transactions involving complex hardware, software, and related services. Most of these differences will be resolved amicably; others may require the intervention of a third party. When these differences are addressed through an adversarial process in the civil courts, the proceedings can be protracted and expensive. Moreover, the outcome is usually decided by a jury with little or no understanding of the technologies involved. Another option—binding arbitration— should be considered as an alternative to litigation and courtroom battles.

When a dispute is arbitrated, the disputants voluntarily submit their differences to an impartial third party whom they have selected. In a process much less formal than a court of law, both sides present their evidence and arguments, and the arbitrator(s) renders a written decision. The parties agree in advance to accept the decision of the arbitrator as final and binding on them. The U.S. Arbitration Act, state codes, and a considerable amount of case law provide the legal basis for arbitration. As such, civil courts are able to enforce arbitration agreements and the awards of arbitrators.[5] The principal advantages of arbitration over litigation are these:

- It is less costly, more expeditious, and less formal than court proceedings.
- The informality and privacy of the hearings promote goodwill, encouraging existing business relationships to continue.

- The parties may choose to select an arbitrator(s) who is an expert in the area of the dispute. (In disputes involving new and complex technology, an arbitrator who understands the technology greatly facilitates the proceedings and an equitable settlement.)
- Because the arbitration agreement is a contract between two parties, they can tailor the agreement terms to their liking. For instance, the agreement could establish the qualifications of the arbitrators, set limits on the award, or establish unique rules for the proceedings.

Recent rulings from the Ninth Circuit Court of Appeals in San Francisco urge caution in binding arbitration agreements. In the case *Prudential Insurance Co. of America v. Lai* (1994) the court overturned a binding arbitration clause because the two employees did not realize that they had waived their right to the full benefits of antidiscrimination laws. In the other instance, the court rejected mandatory arbitration, saying that Arco franchisees may not be "forced by those with dominant economic power to surrender the statutorily mandated rights and benefits that Congress intended them to possess" (*Graham Oil v. Arco Products Co.,* 1994). The caveat for school systems is that they must be certain that the other party is not unduly pressured into the agreement and that they fully understand the rights (e.g., trial by jury) they are giving up.

The American Arbitration Association (AAA)[6] is a nonprofit public service corporation providing arbitration support services throughout the United States. Because the AAA is a well-known neutral, its rules and procedures are widely accepted by courts. Referencing AAA rules in arbitration clauses provides a set of well-tested process rules for reaching quick and equitable settlements without the need for the parties to craft all of the details. The parties also can agree to have the arbitration process administered by AAA and so draw on their nationwide pool of trained, expert arbitrators and their administrative "back office" support.

Another well-known agency for dispute resolution is the Judicial Arbitration and Mediation Services (J.A.M.S.), now known as

J.A.M.S. ENDISPUTE.[7] It differs from the AAA in that it is a for-profit company and all the arbitrators are retired jurists rather than subject-matter experts. Also, a growing number of law firms offer arbitration services on a fee basis. If the parties agree to a binding arbitration clause, it is desirable for the contract to specify the ground rules and how the arbitrators will be selected. Recommended arbitration clauses from both AAA and J.A.M.S. ENDISPUTE are in Appendix E. School boards contemplating use of an arbitration clause in their contracts, of course, should discuss it with their legal counsel and, possibly, with an expert in arbitration.

Notes

1. "Artificial Intelligence" (1994) is devoted to the social issues of computing networks.

2. Appendix B includes a discussion of fair use.

3. Yates and Arne (1994) warn that taking material from outside sources is fraught with legal problems. The copyright laws, as changed in March 1989, provide copyright protection to material even if it has not been registered with the U.S. Copyright Office and even if no copyright notice is on the article.

4. Appendix B addresses copyright issues in some detail.

5. Yarn (1992) is an excellent tutorial on arbitration in theory and practice.

6. The American Arbitration Association headquarters are at 140 West 51st Street, New York, NY 10020-1203.

7. The J.A.M.S. ENDISPUTE headquarters are at 111 Pine Street, Suite 205, San Francisco, CA 94111.

CHAPTER 5

Providing for Technical Support

SYNOPSIS

 Neither computers and networks nor computer users will function long without support from qualified technicians. This support mechanism has four distinct aspects:

1. Support to the users: initial training, encouragement, and problem solving
2. Support to the hardware and software: routine maintenance, recovery from equipment or software failures, and monitoring the work of vendor technicians
3. Administration: inventory control, password and other security administration, software license management, and maintenance of technical documentation
4. Maintaining technical staff proficiency: the half-life of technical knowledge is estimated at 3 years. Formal and informal training is necessary to maintain proficiency with current products and acquire proficiency with new products.

The elements of an effective technical support program are these:

Technical Staff Organization. Trained persons must have specific responsibilities for supporting computer users and for planning, managing, and operating the equipment. Appendix C consists of an organization chart and model job descriptions for all technical staff positions.

Technical Staff Hiring. Hiring truly good people is a difficult task under the best of conditions, and hiring technical staff is particularly difficult if the hiring person is not knowledgeable in that specific technology. University degrees and résumés are of little help. Manufacturers' certifications offer good assurance of competence, but most products do not have certification programs. Absent their own knowledge, administrators hiring technical persons should seek to "borrow" qualified help assessing technical skills.

Outsourcing. This is a viable answer when particular expertise is needed but the hiring of a full-time person cannot be justified. Success depends on both the quality of the vendor and how well the contract is crafted.

Problem Management. The goal of problem management is to return the user quickly to an operational status, analyze problems to discover root causes, and measure user perceptions.

- One key to this is a log of every problem and its resolution; a subsequent analysis of the log will point to underlying problems.
- Another key is a regular survey of the user community to discover how users feel about the support system. Survey results taken in context with the problem log will clarify support staff priorities.
- The other aspect of problem management is monitoring the performance of vendors to ensure that they are meeting their contractual commitments.

Background

Computer and networking technology has progressed well beyond the status of a new-age "toy for technicians." Even so, the best of it has yet to reach the apparently transparent simplicity of the telephone system. It may never get there and, in any case, during the interim the skill and responsiveness of the technical support staff are critical. If they are excellent, problems will be fewer and those problems arising will be resolved more quickly and with much less disruption. If the staff's skills are marginal, the school's experience with computers will be disappointing and unnecessarily expensive.

This chapter is a discussion of the scope of the technical support staff and the central technical support issues.[1] Appendix C contains model job descriptions for the technical staff positions.

Staff and Responsibilities

Staff Roles

One person, the director of technology, must direct and be accountable for the school district's overall technology plan, the execution of the plan, and day-to-day operations. As noted previously, the director should have full decision-making and spending authority for the technical infrastructure, even though the teachers have complete responsibility for how the technology is used in the classroom.

Technical support has four distinct aspects: support of the user community, support of the hardware and software, administration, and technical staff proficiency. In small institutions, all these roles may be filled by a single person, but in larger sites, staff members will specialize even to the extent of focusing only on particular products.

User Support. Users need quick access to technical support, particularly at the outset when they are inexperienced and their confidence is low. Initial user enthusiasm can quickly turn to outright hostility in the frustration of learning to use the new technology. Even the most elementary problems can be daunting to beginners who are overwhelmed by a new vocabulary and even a new way of thinking. One user mailed a photocopy of the floppy disk when a manufacturer's service representative said, "Send us a copy of your disk." Another was baffled by the on-screen command to Press Any Key; "Where is the 'any' key?" the user asked.

Support to users encompasses problem resolution, new product training, and training of new employees. The training has two distinct orientations: technical and application. The technical training deals with how to make the machines and software function and how to resolve routine problems. The application training, however, addresses how this technology can be integrated into the curriculum and used in the classroom. Both the technical and application aspects entail an underlying element of applied psychology, because one objective of the help center is to give the user the self-confidence and knowledge to apply the new technology creatively. Some have found that the user support positions are often most effectively filled by experienced teachers with a flair for computers—they quickly pick up the technical knowledge and, significantly, they have credibility in the teaching community.

In theory, as technology improves and users become more adept, user support needs will diminish. However, school superintendents should not anticipate that this will happen soon. Instead, support costs may increase as a result of greater network and workstation complexity.

Equipment Support. Although conveniently overlooked by both hardware and software vendors, support of technical products is always a cost, albeit a hidden cost, of every purchase. Every box of electronics, length of cable, or item of software has some requirement for skilled technical maintenance. This maintenance can be performed either by outsiders at some out-of-pocket cost, by particularly knowledgeable in-house users, or by the school's technical staff. Regardless of how it is provided, this continuing expense must be factored into the economics of every product purchase and lease decision.

The following equipment support positions are most frequently filled by people with strong engineering or computer science backgrounds.

Administration. The tasks associated with keeping the paperwork in good order may not demand great technical knowledge, but they do require care and precision. Administration includes tracking software licenses equipment, managing the security systems, establishing new-user accounts, validating vendor invoices, and maintaining technical documentation and inventory records. In some organizations, updating software on user workstations and routinely filing backups are also considered administrative tasks.

Technical Staff Proficiency. Equipment and software change rapidly, and training for the staff must be viewed as a priority investment. The half-life of technical knowledge is perhaps 3 years; after 3 years, half of an employee's technical knowledge is out of date and useless. To remain effective, technical staff members require an estimated 40 hours of training a year, depending on the scope of the person's responsibilities. Some of this training may be done at the school using local or purchased training materials. Much of the training, however, will be off-site training. Training sources include product vendors, technical schools, universities, and companies that specialize in technical training. Almost all of these must be planned as an expense to the school, and costs can range as high as $400 per day.

Additional sources of current information for technical staff members are trade publications and electronic bulletin boards. Also, professional groups can be helpful through sharing information about common problems and building a mutual support network. The cost of participating in these groups is nominal, and every staff member should be encouraged to become involved in them.

What does it cost to provide an appropriate level of technical support? The cost of technical support can vary widely and largely depends on the complexity and number of different technologies that must be supported as well as the expertise of the users. The

Gartner Group, as reported in the *Wall Street Journal,* estimates that businesses spend 60% of the overall cost of a computer system on training and support of the users (Moore, 1994). Another *Wall Street Journal* article noted that with a distributed (processing) network,[2] 80% of the lifetime cost was maintenance and management (Yoder, 1994). As reported in *Computerworld,* a 1994 International Data Corporation survey found that the ratio of desktop computer users to user-support staff ranged from 40-to-1 to 600-to-1, and after eliminating the extreme cases the average was 225-to-1 (Vijayan, 1995). In industry, the size of the total technical staff (management, clerical, help desk, and other personnel) is often in the range of one support person for every 50 to 150 machines. Schools, however, seem to manage with less support staff; ratios of one support person for 200 to 300 classroom machines are common, but this will probably change as the technical environment in schools becomes more extensive and complex.[3]

Finally, it should be noted that a number of studies have highlighted the lower support labor requirement in environments with fewer, centralized servers as opposed to a greater number of dispersed small servers.

Organization for Support

Software and equipment support should be viewed as consisting of several layers: Each successive layer involves fewer people who have greater expertise and are less accessible to the end user.

The first line of defense is the informal support that users can get from one another. Although officially invisible, this is the layer in which many questions and problems should be resolved. It is the most friendly and certainly the most immediately available. Moreover, teachers are probably the most qualified persons to support instructional software in their own area. Even if it cannot be overtly managed, this informal support structure should be recognized and encouraged by senior officials. It can be facilitated by newsletters and other vehicles to keep those persons who are the most technically proficient well-informed and enthusiastic.

The next support layer is the technical support staff, whose training should enable them to diagnose, if not repair, most hardware, software, and communications problems without recourse to outside help. Where the staff is more than several persons, a natural selection happens. Those with finely honed interpersonal skills will gravitate to working with users and be particularly adept at it. Others will be technical wizards who revel in solving knotty problems. The structure of the organization should capitalize on these strengths. The frontline staff working directly with the users should have offices near those they serve. The heavy-duty technicians should be located at a central site and be on call to assist as needed.

The final support layer is made up of the distributors, value-added resellers (they package hardware with their proprietary software), and manufacturers of the installed equipment and software. Sometimes, this help is provided under product warranties or fixed-price service contracts, but more often it will be billed to the school on an hourly or per-phone-call basis. Because the technical staff should be held accountable for the cost and quality of all maintenance, all requests for outside services should be made through them. Indeed, even when outside technicians are used, the responsibility for a satisfactory problem resolution must still remain with the school's technical staff, who must verify the quality of the vendor's work as well as the user's satisfaction with the result.

If possible, vendor product support should be addressed before the purchase contract is signed. During the contract negotiations, it must be established what after-sale services the vendor will provide, what response times are to be expected, and what recourse is available when the committed service level is not achieved. These agreements must then become part of the written contract. Once the contract is signed, the technical staff monitors all aspects of vendor performance.

Hiring Technical Staff

Hiring staff members who are technically competent can be problematic. This is because assessing the true depth of an applicant's understanding of a product or area of technology is difficult, especially if the interviewer is not experienced with that technology.

University degrees are indicative of broad knowledge but not of proficiency with specific pieces of technology. A résumé lists job titles and descriptions but hardly reveals the applicant's depth of competency.

Professional certifications, however, do provide assurance of both broad understanding and practical knowledge in a specific discipline, as demonstrated by written examinations. The CCP (Certified Computer Professional)[4] designation is a well-recognized competency appellation for systems developers, programmers, and information management. The A+ Service Technician[5] designation is rapidly becoming a de facto standard; many leading computer companies require it. Also, a number of companies have training and certification programs. For example, Novell sponsors two programs: Certified Network Administrator (CNA) and Certified Network Engineers (CNE), and IBM sponsors the Professional Server Expert (PSE) program. Other companies with certification programs include Oracle, Informix, and Lotus Development.

Certification programs, however, are not yet universal, and many qualified applicants will not be certified. This poses a dilemma for schools. One solution is for the school to give product-specific written tests (available from commercial sources) to applicants. These tests cost from $100 to $500 each but often can be acquired on a site license basis. Another alternative is to "borrow" a knowledgeable person to conduct the technical assessment part of the interview process. Written tests can be both hard to find and expensive, and borrowing people is awkward. However, the penalty for a hiring mistake is often a marginal employee who may be difficult to discharge. Some companies that license tests to assess technical knowledge are the following:

Bookman Consulting, Inc., New York, NY

Computer Training and Support Corporation, Livonia, MI

Individual Software, Inc., Pleasanton, CA

Know It All, Philadelphia, PA

SHL Kee Systems, Inc., Columbia, MD

In addition to satisfying short-term needs, temporary employees can be brought in as a way of screening the skills and work habits of persons before making them an offer of employment.

Student Assistants

Students should not be overlooked as a source of technical skills. Many are well qualified to help with the routine technical support tasks. Schools that use student assistants testify that the students gain useful experience and derive considerable satisfaction as well. Yet regardless of their level of expertise and enthusiasm, student assistants must be supervised by an accountable person.

The use of student assistants should be viewed mainly as a learning experience for the student and not as a substitute for an employee.

Outsourcing

Outsourcing is a contractual arrangement that a school could establish with a supplier whereby the contractor would take responsibility for tasks that would otherwise be done by school employees. For instance, some schools have outsourced cafeteria operations, and others have contracted with janitorial firms.

As the complexity of computers and networks has escalated, a growing technical support industry has arisen. A wide variety of services are offered, ranging from over-the-telephone assistance to dedicated on-site personnel; the suppliers range from small proprietorships to the nation's largest corporations. Schools should not neglect opportunities to consider outsourcing some aspects of their technical support. Prime tasks for examination would be those requiring particularly high levels of expertise in which a full-time person would not be fully used by the school.

If the school chooses to outsource some support tasks, the qualifications of the vendor and the contract terms are critical. A well-drafted contract with a well-qualified vendor is the basis for an arrangement that both parties will find profitable. A poorly drafted contract will be an expensive nightmare. Therefore, if the school is not experienced in this type of procurement and nego-tiation, they would be well advised to enlist outside assistance.

Problem Management

Many user questions and problems are resolved with help from coworkers and without recourse to the technical staff. However, when this informal assistance fails or is not available, the technical staff must always be available to handle user questions and problems during working hours. From the user's perspective, the requirement is simple: Make it work—now! The standard of performance for the technical staff should be "The First Is The Last"; that is, the first phone call to the staff should be the last phone call a user has to make.

When dial-in access to the school's network is available, both employees and students with computers at home will begin to access their files, library resources, and other services by modem. As dial-in use of the network facilities mounts, there will be increasing pressure from these off-premises users for technical support. This may require the technical staff to work the tele-phones in the school's technical center evenings and weekends. Of course, when the activity level is minimal, it may be feasible to have a staff member stand by the telephone at home.

Whenever the technical staff becomes involved in problem resolution, regardless of the nature of the problem, the priority must be to bring immediate assistance to the users. This means preservation of the integrity of the user's data and then restora-tion of the user to an operational status. Only after these damage control steps are complete should the technicians address funda-mental repairs and the causal factors. Also, there should be a policy that the first person the user contacts should take owner-ship of the problem until it is finally resolved to the user's satis-faction. Although others may help in the resolution process, that responsibility never shifts.

PROBLEM LOG

	SET-UP			RESOLUTION		CLOSE
Date/ Time	Client Name/Phone	Problem Description	Resolution Responsibility	Date/ Time	Actions Taken	Date/ Time

Figure 5.1. Log Tracking Resolution of All Problems

The user support function cannot be effectively managed without an understanding of what is happening. Processes must be established to gather and analyze routinely both quantitative and qualitative information about user support. Both are necessary: The quantitative data summarize what has happened and the qualitative data describe how users feel about what has happened.

Accurate problem tracking is both the basis for day-to-day management of user support and the source of data for later analysis. Problem tracking entails maintaining a record of each request for support and the chronology of the problem's resolution. A problem log format similar to that in Figure 5.1 will provide operational data and also the analytical information needed to assess vendor performance, plan technical changes, and schedule refresher training for users.

The qualitative assessment of the user support function only can be made by the users themselves. Regularly, a sample of the user community should be surveyed and asked to rate the support system. The results from a single survey will be of some use, but the trends from a series of surveys can be the most enlightening. Analysis of the problem log in conjunction with the user surveys will both identify problem areas and suggest remedial strategies that reflect the users' priorities. Equally useful, a regular reporting scheme will reveal whether the remedial actions taken achieved the desired results.

A byproduct of a regular survey program should not be discounted: If the survey results lead to visible, well-publicized changes, users may come to believe someone cares. Of course, the risk is that users will become downright resentful if changes are not forthcoming. Moreover, any survey program should be part of an overall teacher and staff communications program that reports back to the users the survey findings and actions planned.

Technical Staff Responsibilities

Central control of software distribution is the only feasible way to ensure that critical and common-use software is kept current. If some machines are allowed to drift away from the current software versions, compatibility and technical support problems begin to creep in. Support from the school's staff will become progressively more difficult; also, the manufacturers lose interest as the gap between the extant software and the current version widens.

The technical staff should be responsible for the installation of the school's standard software suite before the machines are turned over to users. The staff then must maintain the standard suite at the current revision level on all machines throughout the school system. If a network has been established, changes to the standard suite should be distributed automatically over the network to all connected machines.

Within a classroom it is desirable if the software on all machines is identical. The technical support staff should encourage teachers to configure a standard set of applications for the class on floppy disks that can be copied onto each machine in the classroom. As need be, the technical staff should assist the teachers in building the applications software set for their classroom. As mentioned earlier, if it is technically feasible, this software is best delivered and maintained over the network.

As their machine population grows, districts should consider having some of their technical staff trained in equipment diagnostics and repair. Not only might the district save money, but less time will be lost than with machines sent out for repair. A few school districts have had members of their staff trained by equipment manufacturers and have established authorized service centers within the district, thus enabling them to buy parts directly from the manufacturer and, equally important, becoming eligible for service bulletin mailings. (Some school districts, however, have considered servicing their own hardware and have found that their costs would be higher than prices bid by reputable computer support companies.)

If there is sufficient knowledge within the technical staff, they also should evaluate products considered for purchase. As a minimum, this evaluation should assess the product's compliance with the district's technical standards and include testing the product's performance in a realistic environment. An internal evaluation is the most effective means for deciding whether new products will satisfy the needs of the buyer, are compatible with already installed technologies, and are maintainable by the staff. In summary, the following are the responsibilities of the technical support staff.

- Technical support: Maintain and, optionally, repair all authorized computer and communications equipment and software within the school district. Receive all reports of malfunctioning equipment and take responsibility for problem resolution and interim damage control.
- User support: Respond to requests for assistance from teachers and staff. Support will include both technical troubleshooting and user coaching.
- Training: Train teachers and other staff members to use the network services and common-use software effectively. Also, inform employees of school policies and procedures regarding computers and telecommunications. (Student training is the responsibility of the teachers.)
- Facilities management: Install, operate, and maintain network servers, cabling, switches, hubs, modems, and, if installed, the telephone switch and communications satellite equipment.
- Administer the security system.
- Property management: Maintain a record of all electronic equipment and conduct an annual physical inventory. Maintain a record of installed software. Maintain a record of all wiring and cabling.

- Vendor management: Manage the acquisition of all hardware and software. Handle all requests for vendor service, warranty claims, and complaints about vendors' products or service. Monitor the performance of vendors.

Notes

1. "End-User Training and Learning" (1995) focuses on the challenges and the issues of end user training and learning.

2. Distributed processing is when the processing responsibility for an application is split between the client (usually a desktop machine) and an another machine (called a server), such as a file server or a print server. The client and the server communicate over a network.

3. The complexities introduced by networks are manifest in charges vendors levy for telephone support. IBM's published per-call rate for support of nonnetworked machines is approximately 75% less than for machines that are part of a network.

4. Tests developed by the Institute for Certification of Computer Professionals, Chicago, IL. Prior to 1994, designations CCP (programmers), CDP (management), and CSP (systems development) were used.

5. The program is sponsored by CTIA (Computing Technology Industry Association) in Lombard, IL. Test administration is managed by Drake Prometric, located in Bloomington, MN, which has authorized testing centers in the United States and abroad.

CHAPTER 6

Planning Essential Teacher Support

SYNOPSIS

The creative use of computers in the classroom entails a major change in teaching style. This can be traumatic for teachers with 20 years of success with the "present system." The payoff, however, can be striking; the Carrollton City School District in Georgia attributes a change in their high school dropout rate from 28% to less than 3% to the creative use of computers in the classroom.

Although the benefits of the new technologies may be patently obvious to those already converted, computers can be downright unwanted by those less enthusiastic. It is absolutely essential that the administration and the technical staff ensure that teachers' inevitable start-up problems are minimal and that their initial application is virtually guaranteed to be a success. This will not happen without a support plan.

Formal Support. There must be a formal educational structure: classroom training, workshops, and self-paced, computer-assisted hands-on training. Time must be provided and participation mandatory.

Informal Support. Formal training is an effective way to launch a training program, but it is not sustainable. The informal mechanisms reinforce the formal training and, most important, focus on the problem at hand when the problem arises. Coaching begins where formal training leaves off. The coach is not an in-depth expert but simply a nearby person who is familiar with the problem and willing to help at the time the problem arises. A successful teacher support program will build a "coaching culture."

School administrators must establish a climate for success by giving public recognition to those who excel, and, at the same time, there must be permission to make mistakes. The example of those who first succeed must be amplified into a learning experience for others. However, the greatest incentive to change comes from administrators who are visibly enthusiastic and patient with those trying to change.

Background

The investments in computers, networks, and facilities are valuable only to the extent that teachers accept the technology and capitalize on its capabilities. When this happens, the results can be remarkable. The Carrollton City School District in Georgia attributes the reduction in their high school dropout rate from 28% in 1987 to under 3% in 1993 to the widespread use of classroom computers.[1] Carrollton administrators hasten to add that the change was precipitated not by the machines themselves but by the change in teaching styles enabled by the machines—students became much more actively engaged in the learning process. The implications of the Carrollton experience cannot be overstated: Computers are a critical element, but the benefits accrue only when the teachers capitalize on them to involve students directly in the learning process.

The benefits of the new technology and the new teaching model are self-evident to those already converted; others, however, see the transition as unwelcome and threatening. Many might paraphrase Ogden Nash—technology might have been all right once, but it has gone on far too long. It is essential, therefore, that schools have in place a support structure to help with the inevitable start-up difficulties and virtually guarantee teachers success in their initial applications. "Easy to use" is more advertising puffery than a term descriptive of most software, and even those most technically adept occasionally will need assistance.

In classrooms and laboratories, students naturally will turn to their teachers for help with hardware and software difficulties. Teachers must be trained to handle routine questions, and, in addition, teachers must be provided prompt backup by qualified technical support persons.

Teachers Unions

Union Perspective

At the national level, the National Education Association (NEA) and the American Federation of Teachers (AFT) teachers unions are supportive of the use of computers in the classroom, and the NEA has been particularly articulate. The *NEA Resolutions* cites "the critical need to prepare all students to become information-literate adults and responsible citizens." The NEA's position recommending the use of technology in the educational process is clear:

> Technology increases the opportunity to reduce educational inequities within and among schools and school districts. The Association believes that local associations should support efforts to improve the quality of instruction in local schools, to enhance the working conditions of their members, and to protect members' rights. The Association further believes that technology should be used to enhance the roles and instructional opportunities of education employees. (National Education Association, 1994, pp. 40-43)

The NEA also makes explicit implementation recommendations:

- Teachers must be directly involved in all aspects of technology planning, implementation, and subsequent evaluation.
- Teachers must be given training in the use of technologies, materials, and instructional strategies. In addition, they must

be given access to technology, encouragement, and time to integrate technology into the approved curriculum.

Although supportive of the concept of classroom computers, neither union has yet taken positions on such resultant human issues as health, safety, privacy, and intellectual property. One national union official acknowledged that these issues exist but stated that they would be addressed in local bargaining. The official went on to say that their present concerns were more about getting computers into the classrooms than about the follow-on consequences. To understand the positions that teachers unions are likely to take, school administrators must look elsewhere.

9to5, National Association of Working Women, is an effective and vocal advocate for office workers, many of whom intensively use desktop computers or computer terminals. Reflecting this reality, 9to5 has researched available literature and has published "Fact Sheets" that describe prevalent office hazards and recommend remediations—topics range from stress management to air quality. Similar to Canadian and European trade unions, 9to5 has been particularly concerned about the extensive use of CRT displays, especially by pregnant workers. Several of their "Fact Sheets" address the ergonomic and radiation issues incident to CRT use (9to5, n.d.-a, n.d.-b, n.d.-c). Although their recommendations for the safe use of CRTs are not directed to teachers, school administrators should view the 9to5 recommendations as representative of positions that teachers unions are likely to take in the future. In respect to CRTs and their use, 9to5 recommendations closely parallel the suggestions in earlier chapters of this book.

School Board Perspective

Machiavelli observed,

> It must be considered that there is nothing more difficult to carry out, nor more doubtful of success, nor more dangerous to handle, than to initiate a new order of things. For the reformer has enemies in all those who profit by the old order, and only lukewarm defenders in all those who would profit by the new order. . . . Thus it arises that on every opportunity for attacking the reformer, his opponents

do so with the zeal of partisans, the others only defend him half-heartedly, so that between them he runs great danger. (Machiavelli, 1513/1952, p. 55)

School boards need all the defenders they can muster to bring about this change in the classroom. As proponents of reform, the boards already have sufficient enemies; they must make the teachers unions an ally in this technological revolution. If ignored, the union can impede change or through benign oversight not facilitate it.

Teachers anticipating computers in their classroom are certain to have many concerns. Understandably, they will be anxious about job security, health and safety, training, and the unknowns of change itself. Their union will reflect these feelings and may well distill them into a long list of labor-management issues. In the face of union rank-and-file apprehension, working through the issues list can be a protracted, arduous process for school administrators.

On the other hand, the union can be a positive, enthusiastic force for change. To a large extent, the reaction of the union to school board plans for classroom computers will be determined by the school's planning process. Senior school administrators must involve union leaders in the planning process from the very beginning and in the subsequent implementation and evaluation phases as well. A partnership for change must be struck with the union and the teachers' concerns made a prerequisite of change. Where teachers unions have a partnership with the school's administration, the unions have been effective in creating an environment open to change and in directly facilitating change.

As the foundation for this partnership, school boards must clearly affirm that classroom technology is not about job security, that the new technology will not change the overall student/teacher ratio but instead will open new avenues of professional specialization. The discussion about technology in schools must be framed in terms of professional productivity. In a number of ways, it will make better teachers:

- Technology will assume many administrative and housekeeping chores for teachers and so provide them more time to teach and prepare to teach.

- Technology will make available to teachers a wealth of new teaching materials and techniques.
- Technology will directly involve the student in the learning process by providing more hands-on opportunities.

Formal Training

Background

A formal training program for teachers must consider four areas: the technical environment, operating procedures and policies, instructional software, and the learning curve.

Technical Environment

Formal training is especially needed for new employees and also when significant changes are introduced into the technical environment, which includes desktop computers and the school-wide standard software such as the operating system, word processor, and electronic mail. Training sessions should be scheduled so the teacher can put the new skills to use when the training is complete. Under the best of conditions, formal instruction and initial usage of the new skills by the teachers are integrated so that theory and application are combined. School administrators must provide time for this training, competent instructors, suitable facilities, and, most important, they must ensure participation. Few teachers want to risk failure in front of a class when they feel uncertain about new technology. A fundamental aspect of teacher training, therefore, is encouragement and time to practice what has been learned.

Much of the formal training probably will be in the form of workshops conducted by the school's technical staff. Other options exist, however. Companies and consultants who specialize in training individuals and groups in popular products are amply available, and many will conduct their programs at their customer's site. Also, some software vendors provide formal training classes or sell self-paced tutorials and videotapes. If vendor training is considered, it should be addressed as part of the initial purchase agreement; a package deal often can be negotiated.

One industry expert has recommended self-paced video training with concurrent hands-on practice. He observed that it was especially effective for people who are too busy to devote whole days to training. A room was set up with several video units, headphones, and workstations; employees scheduled themselves at convenient hours. Employees also were loaned the video-training tape and a laptop computer so they could take the course at home. A large hotel chain found that video-based training was ideal for those who did not get computer training in school—employees did not feel threatened because they could learn in the privacy of their own homes.

Operating Procedures and Policies

Some formal training, especially for new employees, should be devoted to the school's technical policies and operating procedures. Those school policies dealing with security, privacy, intellectual property, and inappropriate information should be given particular attention. The media center director should discuss the materials available within the media center and those accessible through the network and describe the assistance available to teachers. Also, the director of technology should discuss the technical support process and possibly introduce technical staff members.

Instructional Software

The training required by instructional software packages such as Broderbund's *Where in the World Is Carmen Sandiego?* or IBM's *Writing to Read* is different than training required by complex products such as WordPerfect. Instructional software is usually simpler, smaller, and has a singular focus. Rarely is formal training available; teachers are on their own to understand the product and discern how best to apply it from the basic documentation provided. In the course of a year, a teacher may use many different instructional packages, and attempting to gain expertise in all of them can be overwhelming. It is effective, sometimes, if a group of related teachers works together—each taking a different product to master and then helping the others with it.

Learning Curve

In business offices, it takes 6 to 8 keyboard hours for a new computer user to acquire sufficient skills and confidence so the machine does something the user finds useful—the crucial threshold. Once that threshold is crossed, the machine will be used, and, in time, the user will extend its use to other functions of interest. Though this initial threshold can be reached rather quickly, it can take some years to integrate the capabilities of the computer fully into one's work style. Indeed, Roy D. Pea, Dean of Northwestern University School of Education and Social Policy, has noted that 5 to 7 years are required for a teacher to become comfortable and truly innovative using computers in teaching (Dolan, 1994). A study of technology integration in Westchester County, New York, colleges suggests "that the time for 'real integration' can be shortened to under 5 years with adequate support—including training, equipment, and concerns-based management on several different levels" (Mow & Freweouf, 1994, p. 13).

In summary, formal training is essential but is just the beginning; proficiency goals and the infusion of technology into the curriculum will not be reached without motivation, time to practice, and a patient, supportive environment.

▓ Informal Support

Coaching

Coaching begins where formal training leaves off and is central to success. Because it is neither scheduled nor structured and usually is one-on-one, it is easily overlooked in planning a school's technical support function. Because most problems are rather simply resolved, a coach does not need to be an in-depth expert. It is only necessary that the coach be familiar with the problem at hand and willing to help.

Whereas formal support processes are staffed by technicians, informal support is a grassroots process. Informal support is the as-needed coaching and incidental encouragement from colleagues. This informal support can be fostered with unstructured communications tools such as electronic bulletin boards and brown-bag lunch-time discussion groups. Certainly, the best way to enhance coaching effectiveness is through standardization; if everybody is using the same system, the likelihood that a nearby associate can help is enhanced greatly.

The coaching role is not limited to teachers helping one another, of course. The coaching style should be adopted by the technical support staff when working with the user community. If assistance is delivered with patience and is directed at solving the problem at hand, users will be inclined to ask for help rather than muddle through what is at best a frustrating process.

Enticement—The Hidden Hand

Rational persons will not adopt a new technology until, in some way, they believe it will make them happier, richer, and more satisfied—in other words, will make their life better. Similarly, the migration of teachers from their current teaching mode to the new is determined, to a large extent, by how they perceive the change will affect the quality of their work life. Only when the personal benefits become clearly apparent will the technology be readily accepted.

The school must take the initiative to make the benefits apparent to every teacher. It would be helpful if teachers were provided a software package to make painless (or almost so) all the administrative chores burdening them. Attendance records, report cards, handouts, lesson plans, and tests would all be candidates for this application. The first computer into the classroom should be furnished with this software and go on the teacher's desk.

Credible role models are a fundamental incentive for people to try something new. The best role models are homegrown because they are "just like me and if it works for them it will surely work for me." Exemplary teachers within the school system must be sought out and encouraged. There should be public recognition and tangible rewards for those who excel; at the same time, there must also be a clear permission to make mistakes. The example and the zeal of those who first succeed must be amplified into a learning experience for others.

As previously noted, vehicles for sharing information among teachers are effective tools for building enthusiasm. This can be as simple as a periodic newsletter-style forum for interchange of ideas, success stories, and helpful hints. Workshops, electronic bulletin boards, and demonstrations are other proven tools.

Probably the greatest enticement to taking the risk of change is senior administrators who are both visibly enthusiastic and patient with those striving to change. In fact, it would be impossible to envision success without this kind of leadership.

Note

1. Interviews in 1994 with Dr. Phyllis R. Mitchell, Media Coordinator, Carrollton City Schools and Robert Hendrick, Director of Technology, Carrollton City Schools. The statistics were confirmed by memorandum from Robert Hendrick.

CHAPTER 7

A Success Story

SYNOPSIS

The school system of DeKalb County, Georgia, has become an acknowledged leader in the effective use of technology in public education. This is hardly an overnight success; rather, it is the aggregation of many small success over 20 years. In 1976, a committee led by Frank Barber, then a high school mathematics teacher, drafted a long-range plan to implement a vision of how technology would shape the classroom for the next 10 years. The concepts, objectives, and the plan were accepted by the school board, and Barber was given the job of making it happen. With the assistance of a small staff, the school district's technology program is still managed by Barber.

Success has been a three-legged stool. The first leg is leadership. Since the beginning, Barber has crisply articulated how technology will improve the education of DeKalb's children and buttressed this concept with a plan of incremental steps to achieve it. By dint of his persuasiveness and political acumen, the senior school officials and the school board have enthusiastically accepted the image of the future he has projected, and they have consistently approved the plans for extending technology.

The second leg is public support. Month after month and year after year, senior school administrators and school board members have delivered the message of technology to teachers, parents, and the general citizenry of DeKalb County. There are now few people in the county unaware of the need for technology in the classroom and of how it will improve the education of their children. Indicative of the effectiveness of this missionary work is that the last school bond issue passed by a two-to-one margin in a community that is hardly wealthy—per capita income is 16% below the U.S. average for metropolitan areas.

The third leg is management. The technology program has been managed with skill. A visionary concept, the technical architecture, and the plan have been the basis for each step taken; a highly qualified technical staff has been assembled, and technical standards have been put in place. At every opportunity the message— concept, rationale, and action plan—has been delivered to the school's staff. And, most important, training has been a high priority.

Has it worked? Test scores of students who stay within the school district are trending up. Also, in a community with an increasingly urban, transient population, the school system has not seen the expected increase in truancy and behavioral problems; this is attributed to classroom technology as well as other programs. More telling, however, is obvious student enthusiasm and the caliber of written papers and science projects.

The Story

DeKalb County, Georgia, has a striking success in its school system. The use of computers and telecommunications to enhance its academic program has attracted national attention for both its creativeness and its results. This has been done without wealthy corporate benefactors or special state grants, and it has been accomplished by a community that is hardly extraordinary in other ways. In some respects, DeKalb schools are an unlikely candidate for success because the DeKalb school system, with 82,000 students and 100-plus schools, is big enough to be unwieldy, and DeKalb is a county in a demographic transition.

DeKalb County is an integral part of metropolitan Atlanta, an area with an exploding population. As the city of Atlanta has overflowed its boundaries, DeKalb, which abuts it, has changed from the suburban bedroom community of 20 years ago to an urban extension of the city. In that period, the population has increased by a third, the white majority has shrunk from 85% to 55%, and as the population has become more transient, the percentage of homes owned by the resident has declined almost 15%. In many communities, these demographics would presage an increase in school system problems: truancy, dropouts, discipline, and falling test scores. None of these have happened, and although tracking test scores in a transient population is imprecise, the test scores of those who remain in the district are rising slowly. There is a general consensus that classroom technology has been a major factor; the technology has made the curricula more individualized and the students more actively engaged in the learning process.

These successes are most certainly a collaborative effort, yet at the core there is always a single innovator—one individual who has truly made it happen with a timely idea, persuasiveness, and persistence. In DeKalb County this was a mathematics teacher named Frank Barber, a would-be engineer who turned to teaching "because that is what I always wanted to do" (personal communication, 1995). Equally fortuitous, Dr. James Hallford, District Superintendent, has been Barber's champion for the use of technology in education. Hallford (personal communication, July 20, 1995) has described his role: "One of my principal responsibilities is to create an environment in which technology can flourish."

In 1976 Barber asked to lead a microcomputer committee assembled to look into the potential use of computers in classrooms and to develop a technology plan for the school district. With Hallford's encouragement, the school board approved the plan and put Barber in charge of implementing it. Barber has never returned to the classroom, but, as Executive Director of Management Information Systems, he is still the consummate teacher. Now his students are teachers, school administrators, school board members, and, most important, any county resident who will sit still long enough to listen to him. The vision he has projected and his salesmanship are evidenced by a school board that is pushing him to accelerate the program.

Although Barber's role has been pivotal, were there other success elements that can serve as a model by any school system? Interviews with members of his staff, school administrators, and the deputy superintendent revealed a pattern that was unusual—not because it was bizarre but because it was so sensible. Wittingly or not, Barber, Hallford, Superintendent Dr. Robert Freeman, and the school board have followed the textbooks on making organizational change. Some of this is evident in the milestone chronology that follows, but other aspects bear elaboration, and, as expected, there is no single success factor; rather, it is the intersection of a number of small things done right.

Success was not a happenstance. Since 1976, Barber always has provided a vision and a plan; endorsed by the school board, the concept and the plan were the basis of a continuous dialogue with the teachers and the community. Also, there was an insistence on buy-in and training at every step of the way. In 1980, installation of classroom Apple computers began, but a school could not get its machines until the principal attended 10 hours of training and the computing specialist (the teacher who would teach the other teachers) 50 hours of training. One school did not get any machines until the principal retired.

Today, technology training requirements are even more stringent. In each school there is a computing specialist, a certified teacher who instructs teachers in the use of technology, and a technical specialist who keeps the technology working. The computing specialists get 50 hours of training each summer. The technical specialists receive 4 hours of training monthly and 50 to 100 hours of training in the summer that concludes with a final exam. In addition, administrative personnel are trained on the software and district-unique applications that they routinely use.

Barber says this about training:

> It is easy to bring a bunch of people together and to give them a kernel of knowledge, but that does not change their behavior. They must also be given the incentive to change and the time to develop

the new skills. Ten percent will almost instantly assimilate the technology and become aggressive innovators. Ten percent are DNR—only death 'n retirement will solve their problem. Eighty percent are teachable because they have a child-shaped void in their heart. If you can show them how what you are doing fills that void, and it is good for the children, they will follow you to the ends of the earth. They will work their fingers to the bone. (personal communication, 1995)

Since Barber was assigned in 1976 to implement the technical plan, Freeman and the school board have supported a strong technology office at the district level. This office has been charged with not only implementing the plan but also setting the vision and developing the overall strategic plan. (It is noteworthy that tactical and implementation planning has been decentralized to the principals and computing specialists in each school.) Barber's district-level staff has built a technical architecture and a framework of operational policies and processes that ensure a cohesiveness of the independent activities in the many schools and classrooms.

His staff organization parallels that of each school: Charlotte Curran, Director of Instructional Technology, is more or less the counterpart of the school computing specialist, and Bette Swilley, Technology Coordinator, is a counterpart of the paraprofessional technical specialist. If Barber's role is the visionary and front man, then Swilley and Curran make it work. As did many of his staff, both had experience as classroom teachers before being recruited by Barber. As he said, "It is easy to spot those that are aggressive and have an instinct for technology—those are the ones I go after" (personal communication, 1995).

In the late 1970s, the DeKalb schools adopted a program of continuous progress—students progress through the established curriculum at their own pace. As Curran (personal communication, July 13, 1995) reflects, "I saw the possibility of the computer making continuous progress workable rather than a management nightmare for teachers." Today, her focus is on the use of technology to individualize the learning experience of each student and, more recently, to make it a hands-on experience as well.

The technical architecture developed by the staff (an overview of the network topology is at the end of this chapter) established the standards for new hardware, software, and network acquisitions and influenced the design of new buildings. It also established bridges to the older technologies to extend their useful life. Equally important, the standards it imposed enabled the district to achieve substantial economies of scale in the acquisition of hardware and software and also to negotiate favorable contracts for equipment maintenance and other services. Often the bids are well below the state contract available to schools. Swilley, who manages district technical procurement, routinely challenges prospective vendors to beat the state contract. Procurement centralization set the stage for a program that manages vendor performance. Contracts are written with explicit performance-level criteria, and these criteria then become the standards against which the vendor is evaluated. All calls to vendors for service are made through the central office; the time of the call to the vendor is logged and the problem tracked until it is resolved. Vendors failing to meet the agreed-on performance standards are made aware that future school business is at stake.

Standardization of the technology also has had other benefits. It has made districtwide, technology-based curricula and districtwide training possible. It also has reduced the complexity of the technical environment significantly. This has enabled DeKalb to support its 5,500 teachers and 18,000 computers with a staff of approximately 260. Sixty are employed at the district central office, and the others provide on-site support at each school. One hundred of the on-site personnel are full-time technical specialists, and 100 are computing specialists—teachers who spend part of their day coaching other teachers on the use of technology.

School principals Tracy Moore of Clifton Elementary School and Mary Ann Schrecengost of Cedar Grove High School have no doubt that the technology has improved the educational process. Although both have seen only small improvements in standardized test scores, they cite other indicators: better written papers and a better grasp of the principles of mathematics and science. Equally important, they say, are the instances of the engagement of otherwise disinterested students in the educational process. "When you have to kick the kids out at the end of the day, you have gotten somewhere."

Yet for all their enthusiasm, both principals are concerned about teacher training. They regretted that technology training had not been an even higher priority earlier, and now that it is getting attention, they are not sure how the teachers will find the time for training and mastery. Schrecengost thought that in 5 years there would be a computer on every desk in her school, but she wondered how well the teachers would assimilate the new teaching paradigm and how quickly they would be able to employ the technology creatively.

The principals also are concerned about their facilities. They explained that their classrooms are not suited for computers on a large scale: electrical power, network connections, air conditioning, desks, and room size are all seen as problems if machines are on every desk.

What advice did they have for other schools just beginning the technology transition?

Flexible Plans Supported by School Leaders With Technology Directly Tied to Educational Goals. In the beginning there should be broad consensus to a long-term vision that directly relates technology to the educational goals of the school and what happens in the classroom. The school board and the leaders within the school system should be fully committed to the concept and objectives. Then construct a plan that, in small steps, implements the long-term objectives and a plan that can accommodate midcourse changes as new circumstances arise.

Commitment of the Administration. The administrative staff in the schools must be committed to the technology, and early in the game they all must be using it. If the school's leaders are visibly committed, that is a powerful incentive for the teachers to embrace the new technology. Also, as Moore and Schrecengost emphasized, all teachers must be given a clear message that the effective use of classroom computers is no longer optional.

Extensive Teacher Training. It is impossible to provide too much training for teachers, especially at the outset. As computers begin to saturate the school, the time required for basic training will diminish, and emphasis should be shifted to new ways of applying the technology.

Of course the final question is whether it all has been worth it. Barber echoes that test scores are only part of the answer. Part of the answer is visible in the quality of written work and science projects, and he goes on to say that "students in the work/study program are getting office jobs instead of flipping hamburgers. However, the real bottom line is that a technologically competent society is essential for the economic well-being of the country" (personal communication, 1995).

Milestones and Turning Points

1976	*Turning Point*
	The first strategic plan for the use of technology in the school room is created. The 10-year strategy is approved by the school board that funded the first step.
1976	A GE Terminet® terminal, card reader, and modem are installed in each high school. They connected by a dial-up phone line to a Honeywell computer at the district headquarters.
1979	A Digilog® display terminal is installed in each high school, enabling computer output to be displayed so all the class can see what is happening.
Early 80s	The initial apprehension teachers had about computers largely has been dispelled, and many of the teachers are anxious to try to use them in their classes.
1980-1989	As outlined in the 1976 plan, more than 4,000 Apple IIe machines are installed in schools throughout the district.
1983	Conceptual work for what will become the Integrated Learning Program begins—a computer system that will provide an individualized math and reading program. This work is later folded into the activities of the 1987 technical planning committee.

1987   A committee is formed to extend the 1976 plan for district technology. The committee is structured to be inclusive of all viewpoints in the community. It includes these groups:

- State Education Department
- Teachers
- County Board of Education
- School principals
- Chamber of Commerce
- Parents
- Instructional coordinators

1989   The committee completes its report and presents it to the school board. The key recommendations are these:

- A districtwide network must be constructed, and the stand-alone machines must be replaced by machines connected to a buildingwide network linked to the district network.
- Computer-based instructional material, a means of managing the material, and a means of delivering it are required.
- The price tag for the hardware, software, and support staff is $17 million. The regular school tax revenue and the annual allocation from the state are inadequate for the investment to be made, and the committee recommends that another source of moneys be found.

The school board accepts the plan, and it also decrees that the standard district technology would be the PC-Intel microprocessors and DOS.

1990   *Turning Point*

A $100 million bond issue is proposed. The proposed bond includes $25 million for "instructional enhancement" that includes the necessary funding for the new technology. The superintendent and school board members proselytize county commissioners, PTAs, church groups, NAACP, and any community group that will put them on their agenda. Mailings are sent to all residents.

The bond issue passes by a wide margin. Within weeks there are visible changes; new playground equipment is appearing at all schools.

The approved network technology is challenged by a rejected vendor, and the school board retains Arthur Anderson to examine the technical planning committee's rationale. The staff's methodology and conclusion are found faultless, and the work of building the network is started. It is completed in 1995.

The district begins the process of installing four computers in every elementary classroom. Using the network, the machines are able to access the integrated learning system—a system with a database of more than 5,000 lessons organized by objective. The system is able to deliver the prescribed lessons to students, record their progress, and maintain student records for the teacher.

1994   There is a classroom computer for every five students in the school district, and in some classrooms there is a machine on every desk. According to the 1993/1994 Quarterly Education Data, Inc. survey, DeKalb schools rank fifth in the United States in terms of computer saturation.

1995   All junior and senior high school administrative personnel have a computer on their desk. They have been trained in the DeKalb standard software suite (WordPerfect® with GroupWise® electronic mail, Excel®, Access®, and PowerPoint®), and they are all interconnected by electronic mail.

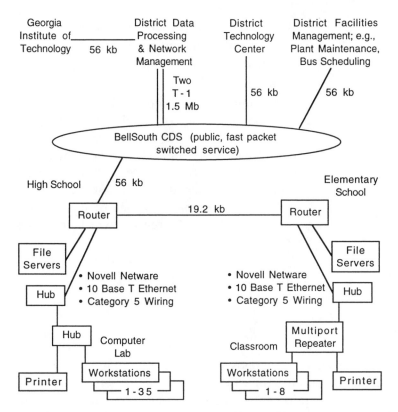

Figure 7.1. DeKalb School's Network Topology

1995   *Turning Point*

The school board approved a strategy for training all teachers, and the board authorized $2 million for technology training systems in three pilot schools. Each system consisted of these components:

- Computer for each teacher's desk
- DeKalb standard suite of software
- A full-motion multimedia, interactive tutoring program that leads teachers to mastery of the standard software

Pilot, a teacher support software system

Twenty portable computers so teachers can pursue their training at home

Support personnel

This training will be done on a school-by-school basis. Once a school has completed training, the program will be moved to another school. The newly trained teachers each will be provided a portable computer and a modem for access to the school's network facilities. Without considering that some teachers may buy their own portables, it is expected that the program will take 3 or 4 years to complete.

1996   An active Internet node is established on the district's network and will be available to all network users.

DeKalb Network Topology

This overview of the network topology (see Figure 7.1) illustrates the broad structure: the use of a public network service, standardized equipment and software at each school site, the subordinate relationship of the elementary schools, and a direct link to the Internet at the Georgia Institute of Technology.

Summary

Education—the transfer of knowledge, skills, and values to youth—must be the highest priority of each adult generation. When this obligation is disregarded, the underpinnings of society begin to disintegrate.

Opportunities to shape the nature of the educational process happen, maybe, once in a century. Computers and telecommunications are providing this unique opportunity in our day. We must avail ourselves of them to improve the overall caliber of learning and to reach students not well served by the present system. If school boards and senior administrators provide intelligent leadership, the assimilation of technology will be both effective and relatively painless; if not, it will be, without doubt, a waste of money and opportunity.

Lest one be misled about the simplicity of the challenge, it is useful to consider industrial experience. Over the past 20 years or so, industries have been using information technology to rebuild their companies to make them more effective in a world economy. It has been and still is a traumatic process; as one chief executive officer said, "Through re-engineering we have saved the business and destroyed the organization." There is a certain semblance between what has been happening in the industrial sector and will happen in the schools. Some elements of industry's experience should be taken to heart by educators and school boards.

- The need to change from the old ways will be rejected by most of the organization, and the means of resistance, whether overt or subtle, will be creative.
- Significant change will not happen without the stubborn insistence and day-to-day visible commitment of the most senior executive.
- Most re-engineering projects that failed did so either because the changes were never really tried or because senior management lacked the fortitude to persevere.

The process of change is not to be taken lightly. Risk is always the handmaiden of change. Managing these risks is the only way to make the possibilities of the new technologies become the realities of tomorrow. Creatively applied, technology will lift the education of our youth to levels heretofore unachievable. The gauntlet is down; the opportunities are boundless.

Power Protection

Sometimes subtle and sometimes dramatic, power disturbances are a frequent source of failure and erratic operation of electronic equipment.[1] These disturbances have many characteristics, and their nomenclature is far from standardized. The following are the most frequently used terms.

Blackouts are periods of no power. Most blackouts are for just a few seconds or minutes and are often caused by lightning storms, vehicle accidents, or overload on the power grid. Their effect is loss of work in process and, sometimes, loss of data.

Sags, undervoltage, and *brownouts* are all periods of low voltage (see Figure A.1). A sag, often defined as low voltage lasting a few seconds or less, is most frequently caused by weather conditions, construction, or traffic accidents. Undervoltage is a period of low voltage lasting more than a few seconds. Brownouts are extended periods of undervoltage caused by power companies reducing the voltage to customers to cope with power demands beyond their capabilities. Low voltage causes unexpected system crashes with associated loss of data and overheated motors.

Spikes are electronic tsunami—very high voltage for a brief instant. They destroy components or, worse, can severely weaken them so they fail, one at a time, over a period of days or weeks after the event. They are most often caused when lightning strikes nearby. Spikes also can result from the switching of large electrical

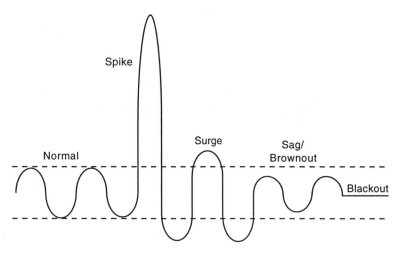

Figure A.1. Typical Power Disturbances

loads either by the utility or the customer. If lightning strikes the cable TV or telephone line, they too will deliver damaging transients to connected equipment.

Surges are increases in voltages lasting at least one cycle. They are most often caused by large electrical loads switching on or off; they also can arise as a secondary effect of lightning strikes. Although surges usually do not have the dramatic effect of spikes, the overvoltage, especially when repetitive, is a cause of premature component failure.

Noise is characterized as low-level changes in voltage in contrast to much larger surges. IEEE Standard 1100-1992 defines noise as a disturbance equal to a small fraction of the system voltage, for example, 3 or 4 volts in a 120-volt circuit. In contrast, a surge is defined as a large fraction or a multiple of the system voltage, for example, 200 volts in an erstwhile 120-volt circuit. When damage is done by noise, it is most often surreptitious changes to the operating system, programs, and data files. These changes can result in immediate system failure or in errors that may not be evident for some time after the incident.

Harmonics are distortions of the sine wave generated back into the power line when nonlinear equipment is attached. Computers, printers, copiers, and machines with variable speed motors are all nonlinear loads and a potential source of problems. Harmonics can lead to erratic equipment performance. More significantly, harmonics can overload the neutral conductor of three-phase circuits, causing overheating and even fires. A school can determine what actions are appropriate only if measurements of the installed equipment are made with a meter measuring true power, including the harmonics; the frequently used clamp-on ammeters understate readings and should be avoided. In addition, schools should insist that new-construction power distribution systems intended for use with computers and other power-sensitive equipment be designed consistent with IEEE Standard 519-1992 guidelines.

In 1994, the IEC (International Electrotechnical Commission) approved a revision to its standard-setting limits on harmonics.[2] The scope of the prior standard has been extended to include most office equipment, including small computers. Although equipment using current less than 220 volts is excluded, manufacturers with European markets will conform to the new standard and, probably, will make the change universal rather than differentiate for the North American market. Over time, the problem will be moderate, but until existing equipment is finally displaced, school electrical systems must be engineered to handle the stress of harmonics safely.

Comprehensive studies of power disturbances have been published by IBM, the National Power Laboratory, and others. However, because of differences in terminology and monitoring thresholds, the reported results are not fully comparable. Figure A.2 is nevertheless representative of the broad picture: The majority of the problems are sags and periods of low voltage, surges and spikes have a significant frequency, and blackouts are infrequent.

Every computer site is subjected to most, if not all, of these possible power problems. They are pervasive and troublesome. When faced with erratic, inexplicable failures, experienced service technicians invariably look for power problems first.

The school board's responsibility is one of balancing the cost of preventing power problems against the consequences of the problem's occurrence. The process is simple. First, determine the

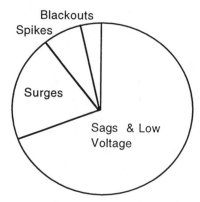

Figure A.2. Power Disturbances

amount of protection needed. The power required can be taken from the nameplates of the equipment to be covered. Nameplate power data often indicate much more power than is actually used in typical configurations; therefore, in installations with many machines, measurements should be taken of equipment at their expected maximum configurations. In addition to the identified demand, adequate provision should be made for future growth; a 25% or larger growth and safety factor often has been used.

Then determine the level of availability desired; that is, the probability that the function will be available when the function is needed. Two factors enter into this judgment: criticality of the applications and number of people affected. A system monitoring the fire and security sensors requires high availability. So does an application directly affecting cafeteria operations. In contrast, the availability required of a single workstation in a computer lab would be lower because other adjacent machines would be available.

In the foregoing analysis, telephone systems, alarm systems, and other life-protecting equipment must not be overlooked. Also, all incoming telephone and cable TV wires should be protected; they too can carry damaging electrical transients and require specialized protection devices.

Table A.1 depicts the types of protection provided by the major classes of power protection equipment.

Table A.1 Power Protection Equipment Characteristics

Type of Problem	Uninterruptable Power Supply	Line Conditioner	Surge Suppressor
Blackout	X		
Sags and Brownouts	X	X	
Surges	X	X	X
Spikes	X	X	X
Noise	X	X	X
Price Range[a]	Thousands $ per circuit	Hundreds $ per circuit	Less than $100 per device

NOTE: a. Within any class of power protection devices, a wide range of products with markedly different capabilities and prices are available.

Power protection always should be approached on three levels: the building's electrical ground, protection at the service entrance, and protection of the equipment.

First, a good earth ground must be ensured. An ineffective ground frequently has been found to be the source of high equipment failure rates and unrepeatable errors. IEEE Standard 1100-1992 recommends an earth ground resistance of 25 ohms or less. Although this may be difficult to achieve in some geographic areas, every effort should be made to achieve the lowest possible reading. This is important for safety reasons as well as for reliable operation of both equipment and power protection devices. The earth ground can be measured with special equipment, a service provided by many electric utility companies. If the quality of the ground is deficient, it should be upgraded before significant investments are made in electronic equipment of any type.

Having established a quality earth ground, a low impedance ground path from each piece of equipment must be validated. Most grounding problems are in the branch circuits. Problems include missing or improper connections and connections worked loose by vibration or repeated heating and cooling. To be meaningful, testing should be done with a ground impedance tester rather than with the common three-light circuit testers.

A surge suppression device should be placed at or near the service entrance to divert lightning and other electrical events originating outside the school. Additional power protection then should be installed close to each piece of equipment. This will protect it from those disturbances that are passed through the service entrance suppressor as well as those generated within the building.

Most surge suppressers include metal oxide varistors (MOVs) that degrade with usage. Suitable surge suppressers should turn off the power when they are no longer effective or at least alert the user when they have failed. Surge protection devices should meet UL 1449. There should be a UL rating for each of the three possible pairs of wires (ground, neutral, and line), and surge suppressors rated at 500 V or more should be avoided. Surge protectors protecting telephone and data circuits should be UL 497A listed.

Notes

1. The Institute of Electrical and Electronics Engineers (IEEE) (1992) provides a comprehensive discussion of electric power for computers and telecommunications equipment.

2. In April 1994, IEC members voted to replace the IEC 555 standard that set limits on harmonics. The new standard, IEC 1000-2-3, became effective January 1996; it covers all equipment rated at less than 16 amperes per cycle and 220 volts or less (i.e., most office and classroom equipment).

Copyright Law and Software

COPYRIGHT LAW

The copyright law (Copyright Act, 17 U.S.C. §106; Software Publishers Association, 1994) gives the owner of a copyrighted work the exclusive right to reproduce, distribute copies, perform, and display the work as well as to make derivative works. However, the protection is not absolute. Under the doctrine of "fair use," portions of a copyrighted work sometimes may be copied without the copyright owner's permission. It is considered fair use if the copyrighted work is used for purposes of criticism, comment, new reporting, teaching (including multiple copies for classroom use), scholarship, or research, and these uses are not an infringement of copyright.

Four factors are considered in determining whether copies can be made in the context of the fair use doctrine.

- The purpose and character of the copying, including whether the use is of a commercial nature or is for nonprofit educational purposes; that is, copying for nonprofit educational uses is more likely to be fair use.

- The nature of the work being copied; that is, copying from works that are primarily factual in nature is more tolerated than copying from creative works.
- The amount and substantiality of the copied portion in relation to the copyrighted work as a whole; that is, the more that is copied, or the more significant the portion that is copied (regardless of the quantity), the less likely that fair use will apply. Note, however, that the copyright holder determines what constitutes fair use, and a few do not acknowledge it at all.
- The effect of the copying on the potential market for, or the value of, the copyrighted work; that is, if the copying has an adverse effect on the market for the original work, it will not constitute fair use.

The legislative history of the Copyright Act of 1976 includes fair use guidelines for educators. Although the "Agreement on Guidelines for Classroom Copying in Not-for-Profit Educational Institutions" is not part of the Act, it has been used by the courts as a persuasive authority as to the extent of copying permitted under the fair use doctrine.

The guidelines provide that a teacher may make a single copy of a copyrighted work for scholarly research, use in teaching, or in preparation to teach a class (e.g., a chart, magazine article, or book chapter).

The guidelines also provide that a teacher may make multiple copies of copyrighted material if the copying meets the following tests and all copies include a notice of copyright:

- Brevity—where the maximum quotation levels, as expressed in number of lines, percentage of whole text, number of drawings, and so on, are not exceeded.
- Spontaneity—where the decision to use the work and the moment of its use for maximum teaching effectiveness are so close in time that it would be unreasonable to secure permission in time.
- Cumulative effect—where used for only one course, no more than one short text or two excerpts are used from the same

author and no more than three from the same collective work. Also, there shall not be more than nine instances of multiple copies for one course during one class term.

The guidelines specifically prohibit copying from works intended to be used in the course of study or teaching, such as workbooks, exercises, and standardized tests, test booklets, and answer sheets. Moreover, copying must not be a "substitute for purchasing books, publishers' reprints or periodicals . . . [nor] directed by higher authority . . . [nor] be repeated with respect to the same item by the same teacher from term to term" (Software Publishers Association, 1994). Copying must not be used to create, or substitute for anthologies or other compilations. In addition, students must not be charged beyond the actual cost of reproduction.

The foregoing constraints notwithstanding, making copies of copyrighted material must be approached with caution. The guidelines are not the law itself; there is no guarantee that, even if the guidelines are followed, the use of copyrighted material will be considered fair use.

School boards should be aware that the Supreme Court has found contributory negligence when "the contributory infringer was in a position to control the use of the copyrighted works by others and had authorized the use without the permission from the copyright owner" (*Sony Corporation of America v. Universal City Studios, Inc.*, 1983). The Center for Governmental Responsibility (1994) speculates that if a school owns licensed software and is authorized to have one working copy, but students become impatient and make additional copies, and the school allows or knows about this, it might be liable for contributory infringement.

Software

When a school acquires software, it actually is acquiring a license to use it from the owner of the copyright; the school does not own it. The conditions and restrictions of the license agreement vary from program to program and should be read carefully.

In general, licenses stipulate that (a) the software is covered by copyright; (b) although one archival copy of the software can be made, the backup copy cannot be used except when the original package fails or is destroyed; (c) modifications to the software are not allowed; (d) decompiling (i.e., reverse engineering) of the program code is not allowed without the permission of the copyright holder; and (e) development of new works built on the package (derivative works) is not allowed without the permission of the copyright holder. The only exception to the constraints of the copyright law are works that are explicitly marked as being in the public domain. Because a copyright notice is no longer required on copyrighted material, the safe assumption is that all creative works are copyrighted unless it is clearly stated otherwise.

Copyright law authorizes civil courts to levy fines as large as $100,000 for each breach of the copyright law. In addition to the copyright law, software is covered by Public Law 102-561, which makes unauthorized software copying a criminal offense. Under this law, software piracy is a criminal offense, and a criminal court can sentence offenders up to $250,000 and 5 years in jail (10 years for repeat offenders).

Rules for avoiding embarrassing legal difficulties can be summarized into four simple rules for handling copyrighted software:

- You may make a copy of an original software program for archival purposes and may make another copy if the original is lost or destroyed. Only one copy of the program may be used at one time.
- You may not load a program onto multiple hard drives for simultaneous use without a license agreement allowing such use.
- You may not load a program onto a local area network server, bulletin board, or disk-sharing system without a license agreement allowing such use.
- You may not use unauthorized copies of software programs or allow a student to make or use unauthorized copies of software programs on school computers.

Information Sources for Schools

The Software Publishers Association (SPA) maintains a hotline (1-800-388-7484) for reporting copyright violations. All reports are investigated, and, if confirmed, appropriate actions are initiated. SPA also publishes copyright information for educational institutions; its material includes flyers, books (including *The K-12 Guide to Legal Software Use*) and a videotape *Don't Copy That Floppy*. For more information, contact the SPA, 1730 M Street, NW, Suite 700, Washington, D.C. 20036-4510; (202) 452-1600.

The U.S. Copyright Office has many publications that are free. Particularly relevant documents are *Circular 92*, which contains the text of the Copyright Act of 1976, and *Circular 21 Reproduction of Copyrighted Material by Educators and Librarians*. Schools should use the Forms Hotline (202) 707-9100 to order specific publications or call (202) 707-3000 to speak with an information specialist. The mailing address is U.S. Copyright Office, Publications Section, LM-455, Library of Congress, Washington, D.C. 20559.

The National School Boards Association (NSBA) has published *Copyright Law: A Guide for Public Schools*. It is an overview of the laws, guidelines, and issues that school districts need to be aware of when setting copyright policy. For more information, contact NSBA, 1680 Duke Street, Alexandria, VA 22314; (703) 838-6722.

The International Society for Technology in Education (ISTE) distributes a number of copyright information resources. One of the publications, *Ethical Use of Information Technologies in Education*, was issued jointly by the U.S. Department of Justice and the U.S. Department of Education in 1992. It focuses on everything from illegal copying to confidentiality and privacy. For more information, contact ISTE, 1787 Agate Street, Eugene, OR 97403-9905; (503) 346-4414.

The Association for Educational Communications & Technology (AECT) publishes a number of books on copyrights, including the following books that would be of use to educators: *Adoptable Copyright Policy* (model policies and manuals for schools), *A Copyright Primer for Educational and Industrial Media Producers*, and *Library Copyright Guide*. For more information contact AECT, 1025 Vermont Avenue, NW, Suite 820, Washington, D.C., 20005; (202) 347-7834.

Model Job Descriptions

OVERVIEW

The following skeletal job descriptions outline the principal technology support responsibilities. They identify the basic activities to be performed in each position and structure the positions into progressive levels of competence and compensation.

Although Figure C.1 implies a ranking of the positions, reporting relationships can take many configurations and are not reflected here. The positions of supervising technology support specialist and senior technology support specialist are essentially the same with the exception of supervisory responsibilities.

Director of Technology

Primary Functions

1. Establish the school district's technical architecture, 5-year technology plan, and the 1-year budget for all computer hardware, software and related support, technical training, and telecommunications services.

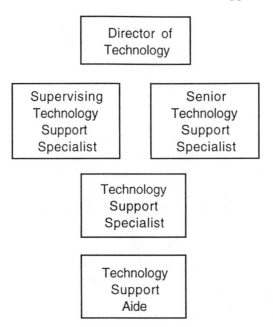

Figure C.1. Technical Support Functions

2. Manage the execution of the plan, day-to-day operations, and user support.
3. Manage the procurement of all hardware, software, and communications services.
4. Provide technical counsel to the superintendent and the school board.

Reports to the superintendent of schools

Subordinate reporting positions: Technical support persons

Responsibilities

• Assessment: Annually apprise the superintendent of the state of the school district's installed technology and the use made of it.

- Architecture: Annually review and update the technical architecture; secure the superintendent's and board's approval of changes made to the architecture.

- Planning: Annually, in consultation with the school district's staff, update the 5-year technology plan. Ensure that this plan supports the school's instructional plan and directives from state education. Based on the 5-year plan, prepare the budget and activity plans for the ensuing year.

- Data security and privacy: Establish and administer policies and procedures for security, privacy, and intellectual property rights; ensure district personnel are well informed about them.

- Operations: Manage the design, installation, operation, and maintenance of all networks. Install, operate, and maintain all central server and telecommunications equipment and software. Manage the installation and maintenance of all computers and associated equipment.

- User support: Provide users with a single point for resolution of all user-perceived problems. Provide 24-hour on-call support when necessary to meet user needs. Ensure that an accurate record is kept of all problems and product complaints, their resolution, and their final disposition.

- Quality measurements: Establish measurements and goals for user support. Provide periodic reports of performance to goals.

- Training: Provide training so district personnel are adequately trained in basic computer skills, network operations, and common-use software. Provide training in the effective application of computer technology. Provide training to ensure that technical personnel can fulfill their support responsibilities.

- Procurement: Manage the procurement of all hardware, software, and telecommunications services. Also manage all requests to vendors for repairs or technical support. Negotiate districtwide site licenses and vendor discounts. Approve all payments for purchases and outside labor. Maintain a record of vendor performance.

- Property management: Establish inventory control of all computer equipment and licensed software.

Education and Experience

- Education: Bachelor's degree in information systems, computer science, or related discipline. An advanced degree is desirable.
- Experience: Twelve years of information systems experience, some of it in end user support. Five years of management experience.

Supervising Technology Support Specialist

Primary Functions

1. Supervise assigned technology support specialists.
2. Provide a high level of technical expertise.
3. Install and maintain computers and associated network equipment.
4. Train users.
5. Resolve hardware and software problems.

Reports to the director of technology

Subordinate reporting positions: Senior technology support specialist, technology support specialist, technology support aide

Responsibilities

- Establish work priorities and supervise assigned personnel.
- Network management: As directed, install and operate all computer network servers and communications equipment (including cabling, switches, hubs, multiplexors, and modems) and also, if installed, telephone switches and satellite communications equipment.
- Technical support: Troubleshoot and maintain all authorized computer and communications equipment within the school district. Maintain a time-stamped log of all service requests and maintenance activities, actions taken, and final disposition.

- Vendor service: Initiate requests for vendor service or re-placement under warranty. Log all support requests to vendors, vendor actions, and final disposition. Log all user product complaints.

- Report generation: As requested by the director of technology, prepare reports of technical support activities and vendor performance.

- Training: Train and coach teachers and staff members in the operation of hardware and software so they can effectively use the network services and common-use software. Provide training to all users in security and privacy policies and procedures. Counsel the teaching staff on the application of technology to classroom situations and, when requested, provide assistance as well.

- Property management: Maintain a record of all electronic equipment and, as directed, conduct an annual physical inventory. Also, maintain a record of all licensed software. Recommend software revision-level upgrades to the director of technology.

Education and Experience

- Education: Bachelor's degree in information systems, computer science, or related discipline. An advanced degree is desirable.

- Experience: Five years of experience in installing, operating, and maintaining networks, hardware, and software. Must have experience with many of the technologies in use. Experience with both direct support of end users and supervision of employees is highly desirable.

- Certification: Certification by the manufacturers of installed hardware and software is desirable.

Senior Technology Support Specialist

Primary Functions

1. Provide a high level of technical expertise.

2. Install and maintain computers and associated network equipment.

3. Train users.

4. Resolve hardware and software problems.

Reports to the director of technology or the supervising technology support specialist

Subordinate reporting positions: None

Responsibilities

• Network management: As directed, install and operate all computer network servers and communications equipment (including cabling, switches, hubs, multiplexors, and modems) and also, if installed, telephone switches and satellite communications equipment.

• Technical support: Troubleshoot and maintain all authorized computer and communications equipment within the school district. Maintain a time-stamped log of all service requests and maintenance activities, actions taken, and final disposition.

• Vendor service: Initiate requests for vendor service or replacement under warranty. Log all support requests to vendors, vendor actions, and final disposition. Log all user product complaints.

• Report generation: As requested by the director of technology, prepare reports of technical support activities and vendor performance.

• Training: Train and coach teachers and staff members in the operation of hardware and software so they can use the network services and common-use software effectively. Provide training to all users in security and privacy policies and procedures. Counsel the teaching staff on the application of technology to classroom situations and, when requested, provide assistance as well.

• Property management: Maintain a record of all electronic equipment and, as directed, conduct an annual physical inventory. Also, maintain a record of all licensed software. Recommend software revision-level upgrades to the director of technology.

Education and Experience

• Education: Bachelor's degree in information systems, computer science, or related discipline. An advanced degree is desirable.

• Experience: Five years of experience in installing, operating, and maintaining networks, hardware, and software. Must have experience with many of the technologies in use and with the direct support of end users.

• Certification: Certification by the manufacturers of installed hardware and software is desirable.

Technology Support Specialist

Primary Functions

1. Install and maintain computers and associated network equipment and hardware.
2. Coach and assist users in the resolution of hardware and software problems.

Reports to the director of technology or the supervising technology support specialist

Subordinate reporting positions: None

Responsibilities

• Network management: As directed, install and operate servers, data network equipment, and voice communications equipment.

• Technical support: As directed, troubleshoot and maintain computer and communications equipment. Maintain a time-stamped log of all service requests and maintenance activities, actions taken, and final disposition.

• Vendor service: Recommend requests for vendor service or replacement under warranty. Log all support requests to vendors, vendor actions, and final disposition. Log all user product complaints.

- Training: Assist and coach users in the operation of hardware and software. Assist users with security and privacy procedures.
- Property management: As directed, maintain inventory records of all installed equipment and licensed software and assist in the physical inventory.

Education and Experience

- Education: Bachelor's degree in information systems, computer science, or related discipline.
- Experience: One year of experience in installing, operating, and maintaining networks, hardware, and software. Experience with some of the technologies in use and with direct support of end users is highly desirable.
- Certification: Network administration certification is desirable.

Technology Support Aide

Primary Functions

1. Assist in the technical support functions.
2. Perform administrative tasks as assigned.

Reports to the director of technology or the supervising technology support specialist

Subordinate reporting positions: None

Responsibilities

- Network management: Monitor central servers. Perform backup and recovery functions for all network servers and, when requested, attached workstations.
- Technical support: Assist in equipment and software installations, upgrades, and problem resolution.
- Administration: Administer user accounts (adding, deleting, assignment of file space, etc.). Maintain hardware and software

documentation library. Administer inventory and other record-keeping systems.

- Training: Assist and coach users in the operation of hardware and software. Assist users with security and privacy procedures.

Education and Experience

- Education: Associate's degree in information systems, computer science, or related discipline or the equivalent in work experience. Active pursuit of a Bachelor's degree is desirable.
- Experience: One year of programming, operating, or maintaining computers and related equipment. Experience in direct end user support is desirable.

APPENDIX D

Policy Templates

Overview

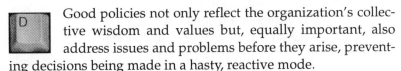 Good policies not only reflect the organization's collective wisdom and values but, equally important, also address issues and problems before they arise, preventing decisions being made in a hasty, reactive mode.

The following 20 policies are neither definitive nor exhaustive. Instead, they are a basis for approaching the central issues this new technology brings to the fore in school systems. They are models for school districts to use in the creation of their own policies, reflecting their own needs, priorities, and biases. Once approved, these policies become the foundation for district operating procedures that should be developed to flesh out responsibilities and describe exactly how the policies are to be applied.

Index of Policies

A. Operations
   A1. Technical Standards
   A2. Passwords, Security, and Privacy

A3. Data Backup
A4. Virus Control
A5. Dial-in Access
A6. Physical Security
A7. Physical and Data Security Violations
B. Administration
   B1. Architecture
   B2. Planning and Budgeting
   B3. Computers and Related Procurements
   B4. Property Control
   B5. Operation and Maintenance of Equipment
C. Other
   C1. Technical Support for Users
   C2. Technical Support for Students
   C3. Equal Access to Computers
   C4. Copies of Data and Software
   C5. Software and Hardware Ownership
   C6. New Plant Investments
   C7. Environmental Inspection
   C8. Access to Inappropriate Information

Policy: A1. Technical Standards

Scope: All computer and telecommunications hardware and software

Statements of Policy

1. Consistent with standards set forth by state education and the federal government, the director of technology shall establish the technical standards and procedures for the school district. They shall be established to promote the interchange of information, ease of use, reduction of maintenance cost, and the facilitation of long-term technical evolution.

2. Without explicit exception granted by the director, all equipment and software procured or otherwise brought into the

school system will be in conformance with the established standards.

▨ Policy: A2. Passwords, Security, and Privacy

Scope: All information in electronic form within the school system

Statements of Policy

1. In the context of this policy, a private password is a secret key, a word known only to the user. Private passwords shall ensure the password owner against unwarranted scrutiny of password-protected information. Private passwords will be used to validate the identity of a user before granting access to any network services or information.
2. The director of technology will make certain all employees responsible for equipment and data are cognizant of their responsibility to protect them from unauthorized use or access. The director will provide and administer the appropriate access control systems.
3. Employees, contractors, and consultants may have private passwords; however, when employment or the work contract or consulting assignment ends, their password(s) will be immediately invalidated.
4. Students may be allowed private passwords at the discretion of the school administration. There may be instances in which a password must be entered to gain access to the system and private passwords are not wanted—for instance, primary school children needing access to a networked printer. Here a public name and password can be given to all who need access. However, this password should be changed on a daily basis.
5. Private data are data protected by a private password or data stored on removable media kept under lock and key. Private data shall be considered private property and not subject to scrutiny without the owner's informed written consent, a

search warrant, or a written order from the superintendent of schools. The school's legal counsel and the owner of the data will be informed of each instance.

Policy: A3. Data Backup

Scope: All data on electronic media

Statements of Policy

1. Responsibility for data protection rests with the "owner" of the data and, unless otherwise specified, the owner of the data is the creator of the data. The owner determines the severity of the consequences if the data are lost or corrupted.
2. Making a backup copy of all data of concern is the responsibility of the owner of the data.
3. The director of technology will make certain that users are aware of their responsibility and will encourage backups to be performed at least daily. The director shall provide appropriate software and backup media.
4. The director will ensure that data on central servers is backed up daily and that the backup copies of critical files are kept in a place safe from flood, fire, or other major catastrophe.

Policy: A4. Virus Control

Scope: All software not procured from authorized sources

Statements of Policy

1. Authorized sources for software procurement are established by the director of technology or by state education.
2. The director will install and maintain virus protection software on all central servers within the school district. The director also may choose to install virus protection on all

machines in the district, but, if this is not the case, all software brought into the school system from other than authorized sources shall be delivered first to the technical staff, who shall ascertain that the software is virus free.

3. When employees or students using home computers have telecommunications access to school machines, every effort will be made to be sure they are not the source of viral contamination of the school's machines. All machines accessible by dial-in computers must have virus protection software.

4. The director of technology will make all employees acquainted with typical virus symptoms and the actions to be taken should a virus be suspected.

5. Persons responsible for intentionally introducing a virus into school equipment, or attempting to do so, shall be brought immediately before the superintendent.

6. Teachers shall make certain that students fully understand this policy.

Policy: A5. Dial-in Access

Scope: Telecommunications access to school networks or free-standing computers

Statements of Policy

1. There shall be no access to the school's networks or free-standing computers via public communications systems until the director of technology has established all appropriate security measures. At a minimum, these measures shall preclude access by unauthorized persons and also prevent those granted access from introducing computer viruses.

Policy: A6. Physical Security

Scope: Computers and telecommunications equipment

Statements of Policy

1. The director of technology shall protect all centralized equipment from unauthorized intrusion, fire, heat, water, damaging electrical anomalies, and magnetic fields.
2. The director shall ensure a continuous source of power for critical electronics such as telephones, alarm systems, and safety equipment. Also, the director will ensure that there is appropriate software and sufficient emergency power for an orderly shutdown of all other centralized equipment in the event of power failures.
3. All protection systems will be tested at least annually.
4. The director shall ensure that electric power delivered to all electronic systems and the electrical ground path meet both the specifications of the equipment manufacturers and the National Electric Code.

Policy: A7. Physical and Data Security Violations

Scope: All breaches and attempted breaches of security protecting computers, telecommunications equipment, and data

Statements of Policy

1. Persons attempting to breach or actually breaching the school's physical or data security shall be brought immediately before the superintendent. If a public law has been broken or it is suspected that a public law has been broken, the superintendent will notify law enforcement officials and the school's legal counsel without delay.
2. In the following circumstances, federal law may have been broken and federal law enforcement officials should be notified:
   - There is reason to believe that there has been (a) unauthorized access of data stored in federal government computers or (b) those of federally regulated institutions (Computer Fraud and Abuse Acts of 1984 and 1986, respectively).

- There is reason to believe that a computer used in inter-state communications has transmitted data, the intent of which is to damage or obstruct a computer, data, or network (Computer Abuse Amendments Act of 1994).

3. If any person has evidence or reasonable grounds to suspect breaches or attempts to breach physical or data security, they shall notify the superintendent without delay.

Policy: B1. Architecture

Scope: All electronic technology and the supporting infrastructure

Statements of Policy

1. Annually, the director of technology will initiate a process to review and, if needed, to revise the technical architecture.
2. The director will validate the extant vision and goals with the superintendent and the school board.
3. The superintendent and key members of the administration and teaching staff will be consulted and their views solicited in respect to the future needs of the school.
4. Taking measure of changes in user needs and in the technical outlook, the director will incorporate the necessary revisions in the technical architecture. These will be presented to the superintendent and board for approval.

Policy: B2. Planning and Budgeting

Scope: All computer and electronic communications hardware, software, personnel, and facilities

Statements of Policy

1. Annually, the director of technology will prepare a 5-year technology strategy and supporting rationale. This will establish a calendar of major activities and milestones. It will

identify funds, manpower, and other resources required to implement the plan. For each major activity, it will identify the success criteria and how they will be measured.

2. The director is responsible for developing a 5-year technical strategy and an annual budget consistent with the technical architecture and supportive of instructional plans.

3. Annually, after the 5-year strategy is approved, the director will prepare an operating budget and activity plan for the ensuing year. This annual plan should be the fulfillment of the first year of the 5-year strategy. The plan will include provision for the following:

- Equipment and software purchases and leases (instructional and administrative software may be included as memorandum items if they are included under other headings in the school budget)
- Equipment and software installation and maintenance expense
- Building modifications (may be included as memorandum items)
- Technical consultants and contractors
- Training for technical staff
- Training for instructional and administrative staff (may be included as memorandum items)
- All telecommunications expense
- Labor and supplies expense for the technical support staff

Policy: B3. Computer and Related Procurement

Scope: All computers, telecommunications, software, and related services

Statements of Policy

1. The director of technology is responsible for managing the procurement of all hardware, software, and related services.

2. The director will qualify all prospective vendors, including technical contractors and consultants.

3. The director also will establish standards for software and equipment to ensure maintainability and compatibility with the existent or planned technology.

4. The director is responsible for the specifications for all central server equipment and all operating system, network, and related software procurements, including standardized, commonly used software such as word processors and spreadsheets.

5. The curriculum director is responsible for the selection of all instructional software and the specifications for academic equipment.

6. The superintendent is responsible for the selection of all administration software and the specifications for administration equipment.

Policy: B4. Property Control

Scope: Computers, communications equipment, and all related software

Statements of Policy

1. The director of technology will maintain inventory control of all communications equipment, computers, related equipment, spare parts, and all software except instructional software. The inventory will identify the version level of software and the configuration of the computers.

2. The curriculum director also will maintain inventory control of all instructional software.

3. The directors will take an annual inventory of all equipment and software and provide a written report to the superintendent. Obsolete or surplus items will be identified and disposition recommended.

4. If surplus or obsolete material is sold or donated, preference will be given to employees and students.

Policy: B5. Operation and Maintenance of Equipment

Scope: Computing and communications equipment and software

Statements of Policy

1. The director of technology is responsible for the operational condition of all of the school district's computer and communications equipment.
2. The director is responsible for the operation of all central servers and all voice and data communications equipment. All equipment and software shall be maintained at current revision levels.
3. The responsibility for academic and administrative software revision-level control rests with the curriculum director and the superintendent, respectively.
4. No equipment may be attached directly to either the voice or data networks without the approval of the director.

Policy: C1. Technical Support for Users

Scope: Support to employees, contractors, and consultants

Statements of Policy

1. The director of technology is responsible for the resolution of all hardware, software, and communications problems.
2. The director shall establish standards of performance for user support.
3. Quarterly, a sample of users will be surveyed to ascertain their perceptions of the technical support received. An analysis of the survey results will be given to the superintendent.

4. The director shall maintain a log of each problem and request for assistance. The log will record the time of the problem or request, contain a description of the problem and actions taken, and the time of resolution.

5. The director shall determine if outside technical support is required to resolve a problem and, if used, shall monitor the performance of the outside technicians until a satisfactory resolution is achieved.

6. The director shall periodically review the problem log, identify problem areas, and initiate remedial actions, including technical staff and user training, replacement of problem-prone components, vendor negotiation, and vendor disqualification. Quarterly, an analysis of the problem log will be given to the superintendent.

Policy: C2. Technical Support for Students

Scope: All students and teachers

Statements of Policy

1. It is the responsibility of the teacher to instruct students in the use of computers and applicable software. It is also the teacher's responsibility to resolve routine student problems.

2. The technical support staff will provide support to the teacher as needed but, under normal conditions, will not work directly with the student.

Policy: C3. Equal Access to Computers

Scope: All students

Statements of Policy

1. All students at any given grade level shall have equal access to computers, software, and computer-based information sources.

2. Access to a computer shall not advantage one student over another. If any student is allowed to use a computer to complete or assist in classroom or laboratory assignments, then all students in the class or group must be availed of the same opportunity.

3. If the use of computers in the homes provides academic advantage to some students, then computers for home use will be provided for all students requesting them.

Policy: C4. Copies of Data and Software

Scope: All software and data regardless of media

Statements of Policy

1. In the context of this policy, the term *software* includes operating systems, compilers, utilities, application programs, databases, extracts from databases, multimedia files, and any other data recorded in electronic media. This definition also includes associated instruction books and reference manuals.

2. Licensed or copyrighted software will not be duplicated except as authorized by the licensor or the owner (or agent) of the copyright.

3. If unauthorized copies are found or suspected, the director of technology shall be notified immediately and shall initiate appropriate remedial actions. The director will apprise the superintendent of any findings and recommendations.

4. When shareware is used within the school system, the director should be informed of each instance and should make the required or appropriate payment to the author. (Shareware is software distributed on a trial basis in which the user is trusted to remit some fee to the author if the program is used.)

Policy: C5. Software and Hardware Ownership

Scope: District employees, contractors, consultants, and students

Statements of Policy

1. The school district has all ownership rights to any software or hardware developed by district employees during their tenure as employees. It does not matter whether the development work was done on school property or during working hours or on personal time.

2. The school district has all ownership rights to any software or hardware developed or researched by consultants or contractors during the hours of their employment. In addition, the school has title to any hardware or software developed by consultants or contractors if the creation is a direct outgrowth of their work for the school and the creation was completed within one year of the termination of services.

3. A student has full ownership rights to any hardware or software developed by the student, regardless of any advice or assistance given by a school teacher, contractor, or consultant.

4. Upon recommendation of the superintendent, the school board may grant monetary awards to employees, consultants, or contractors in recognition of their software or hardware contribution.

5. Software or hardware created by school employees or contractors and owned by the school district is in the public domain. Hardware designs and software items are available to all who request them at some nominal handling charge.

6. Prospective employees, consultants, and contractors may divulge a description of hardware or software they have substantially completed and request an exception from paragraph 1 above. The superintendent may grant such an exception in writing.

7. Upon recommendation of the superintendent, the school board may waive its rights to hardware or software developed by an employee, consultant, or contractor.

8. Any dispute concerning this policy or its terms, including whether such terms are arbitrable, shall be settled by binding arbitration. The arbitration proceeding shall be conducted under the Commercial Arbitration Rules of the American

Arbitration Association in effect when the demand for arbitration of the rules was made. A decision and award of the arbitrator made under said rule shall be exclusive, final, and binding on both parties, their heirs, executors, administrators, successors, and assigns. Each party shall bear its own costs and expenses and an equal share of the arbitrator's fee and the fees of arbitration administration.

9. New employees, consultants, and contractors must acknowledge receipt and acceptance of this policy at the time of hiring.

Policy: C6. New Plant Investments

Scope: Acquisition of new buildings, major renovations of older buildings, and new furniture and fixtures

Statements of Policy

1. It is the responsibility of the superintendent of schools to make sure new and renovated buildings are constructed to be suitable for the technology to be used in the foreseeable future.

2. Specific consideration will be given to each of the following:
   - Adequacy and quality of electric power
   - Availability of electric power and network access at all places where computers or other electronics might be used
   - Adequacy of the heating and air-conditioning system to cope with the demand imposed by the electronics
   - Lighting, seating, and work surfaces suitable for the technology and minimization of ergonomic stress
   - Placement of equipment to minimize student and employee exposure to electromagnetic radiation

3. The director of technology will assist in developing procurement and architectural specifications and make sure that proposed procurements and constructions support the anticipated technologies.

Policy: C7. Environmental Inspection

Scope: Installation of computers, workstations, and computer terminals

Statements of Policy

1. The director of technology shall inspect computer installations and planned installation sites for conditions potentially damaging to the equipment or to the health of the users.
2. Specific consideration will be given to each of the following:
   - Adequacy and quality of electric power and electrical ground
   - Availability of electric power and network access at all places where computers or other electronics may be used
   - Adequacy of the heating and air-conditioning system to cope with the demand imposed by the electronics
   - Lighting, seating, and work surfaces suitable for the technology and minimization of ergonomic stress
   - Placement of equipment to minimize student and employee exposure to electromagnetic radiation
3. The director will inform the superintendent of unsuitable conditions and recommend appropriate actions.

Policy: C8. Access to Inappropriate Information

Scope: Electronic access to material deemed offensive or inappropriate by any person accessing the information and, in the case of students, parents or guardians as well

Statements of Policy

1. Schools officials will forewarn employees, contractors, students, and the parents or guardians of students that they may be offended by material they access by electronic means.

2. Parents or guardians shall be required to sign a consent agreement that (a) the student has been told what is inappropriate, (b) acknowledges the possibility of the student being exposed to inappropriate electronic information—text, graphics, or sounds—and (c) absolves the school of all responsibility if a student is so exposed. If a consent agreement is not on file, a student will be prohibited from using any networked computer.

3. It is not necessary to warn people of specific sources.

4. No employee, contractor, or student using school computers or networks shall knowingly expose persons to material that they will find offensive or knowingly place persons in situations in which they will be exposed to material they will find offensive.

5. Persons exposed to material they deem offensive will inform their teacher or supervisor of the incident. The superintendent will be apprised of all such incidents.

APPENDIX E

Standard
Arbitration Clauses

BACKGROUND

Arbitration clauses are often included in contracts as alternatives to litigation for resolving disputes arising from their fulfillment. This appendix consists of sample arbitration clauses recommended by two institutions that have offices in all areas of the United States. One, the American Arbitration Association, is a nonprofit organization that provides a wide range of alternative dispute resolution services, including trained arbitrators and mediators who are expert in the topic being disputed. The hallmark of the other, J.A.M.S./ENDIS-PUTE, is that all its arbitrators and mediators are attorneys or retired jurists.

The following dispute resolution clauses illustrate some of the arbitration possibilities. Mediation, which offers the possibility of a more amicable resolution, is another possibility and can be a step taken prior to binding arbitration. Dispute resolution clauses are sometimes drafted as a combination of arbitration and mediation processes; a sample mediation clause also is illustrated. There are many options, and schools contemplating alternative dispute resolution measures should seek advice from their legal counsel.

▨ American Arbitration Association Clauses

Existing Disputes

When parties agree to arbitrate an existing dispute, it can be accomplished by use of the following clause:[1]

> We, the undersigned parties, hereby agree to submit to arbitration administered by the American Arbitration Association under its Commercial Arbitration Rules the following controversy: (cite briefly). We further agree that the above controversy be submitted to one (three) arbitrator(s). We further agree that we will faithfully observe this agreement and the rules, and that we will abide by and perform any award rendered by the arbitrator(s) and that the judgment upon the award rendered by the arbitrator(s) may be entered in any court having jurisdiction thereof.

Future Disputes

The following provisions illustrate some of the ways agreements for future disputes can be shaped to meet the needs of the parties.

Standard AAA Clause. Any controversy or claim arising out of or relating to this contract, or breach thereof, shall be settled by arbitration in accordance with the Commercial Arbitration Rules of the American Arbitration Association, and judgment on the award may be entered in any court having jurisdiction thereof.[2]

Clause Providing for Arbitrators' Qualifications. Any controversy or claim arising out of or relating to this contract, or breach thereof, shall be settled by arbitration in accordance with the Commercial Arbitration Rules of the American Arbitration Association, and judgment on the award rendered by the arbitrator(s) may be entered in any court having jurisdiction thereof. One of the arbitrators shall be a member of the Bar of the State of _____ and actively engaged in the practice of law or a retired member of the state or federal judiciary. The other two arbitrators shall have such qualifications, as the parties may agree, as necessitated by the nature of the dispute. If unable to agree on the qualifications of the remaining arbitrators, the makeup of the panel shall be determined by the American Arbitration Association.[3]

Clause Giving Arbitrators Power to Order Document Exchange. Any controversy or claim arising out of or relating to this contract, or breach thereof, shall be settled by arbitration in accordance with the Commercial Arbitration Rules of the American Arbitration Association by a panel of three neutral arbitrators (panel) in the city of _____, and judgment on the award may be entered in any court having jurisdiction thereof.

The panel shall have the authority to order pre-hearing exchanges of information, including and without limitation, production of requested documents, exchange of summaries of testimony of prospective witnesses, and depositions as may be necessary.[4]

Clause Limiting Arbitrators, Power to Award Costs. Any controversy or claim arising out of or relating to this contract, or breach thereof, shall be settled by arbitration administered by the American Arbitration Association in accordance with its Commercial Arbitration Rules, and judgment on the award rendered by the arbitrator(s) may be entered in any court having jurisdiction thereof.

Each party shall be responsible for its own costs incurred in any arbitration, and the arbitrators shall not have the authority to award such costs in its decision. The panel shall have the authority to assess the administrative fees and expenses of the American Arbitration Association and the compensation and expenses of the arbitrators.[5]

Clause Limiting Issues to Be Arbitrated and Limiting the Scope of Relief Arbitrators May Award. Any dispute arising out of the payment of commissions under this contract shall be settled by arbitration in accordance with the Commercial Arbitration Rules of the American Arbitration Association before a single arbitrator, and judgment on the award may be entered in any court having jurisdiction thereof. In connection with such disputes, the arbitrator shall have the authority to order specific performance but shall not have the authority to award punitive damages.[6]

Clause for Mediation Prior to Arbitration. Any controversy or claim arising out of or relating to this contract, or breach thereof, and if said dispute cannot be settled through direct discussions, the parties agree first to endeavor to settle the dispute in an amicable manner under the Commercial Mediation Rules of the American Arbitration Association. Thereafter, any unresolved controversy or claims arising out of or relating to this contract thereof will be settled by arbitration as described in the following paragraph(s).[7]

J.A.M.S./ENDISPUTE Arbitration Clauses

Arbitration Clause. Any dispute arising out of or relating to this contract that cannot be settled by good faith negotiation between the parties will be submitted to J.A.M.S./ENDISPUTE for final and binding arbitration pursuant to J.A.M.S./ENDISPUTE (specify Streamlined, Comprehensive, Employment, or Personal Injury) Arbitration Rules and Procedures.[8]

In the arbitration clause above, *streamlined* refers to rules governing an expedited arbitration process presided over by a single arbitrator. It is only applicable to disputes in which no claim or counterclaim exceeds $250,000, not including interest. The *comprehensive* rules provide the option of a three-person panel, more formal and extended proceedings, and an optional appeal procedure.

For smaller, less complex disputes involving $150,000 or less, there is a short format mediation/arbitration program.

In arbitration and mediation proceedings, there are a few fixed rules. Parties may agree to any proceedings that meet their need. Even though a contract specified the comprehensive rules, circumstances could be such that the parties decide to use the short format.

Mediation/Arbitration Clause. Any dispute arising out of or relating to this contract that cannot be settled by good faith negotiation between the parties will be submitted to J.A.M.S./ENDISPUTE for nonbinding mediation. If complete agreement cannot be reached within _____ days of submission to mediation, any remaining issues will be submitted to J.A.M.S./ENDISPUTE for final and binding arbitration to J.A.M.S./ENDISPUTE's Arbitration Rules.[9]

Notes

1. With permission from the American Arbitration Association. Its headquarters are at 140 West 51st St., New York, NY 10020-1203.
2. Ibid.
3. Yarn (1992), *Alternative Dispute Resolution—Practice and Procedure in Georgia.* Reproduced with permission from The Harrison Company, Norcross, GA.
4. Ibid.
5. Ibid.
6. Ibid.
7. Ibid.
8. With permission of J.A.M.S./ENDISPUTE, Inc. Its headquarters are at 500 North State College Boulevard, Suite 600, Orange, CA 92668.
9. Ibid.

Structured Communications Cabling System—Basic Elements

A structured cabling system is a method of premises (building and campus) wiring designed to minimize life cycle cost, facilitate network administration, and satisfy both current and future technologies. This functionality is ensured through both high bandwidth and an open architecture composed of components meeting widely accepted standards. The following are basic elements of a structured cabling system:

- Equipment subsystem: all of the electronics and hardware in the equipment room and wiring closets. It includes cross-connects, patch panels, repeaters, and fiber-optic connectors.

- Campus backbone: includes the cable connecting the equipment room in one building with the equipment room in another. It also includes devices to protect equipment from electrical spikes and surges when the cable is exposed to lightning. Usually the cable is a first-level backbone from the hub building to the remote building equipment room. Increasingly, fiber-optic cable is the medium of choice for

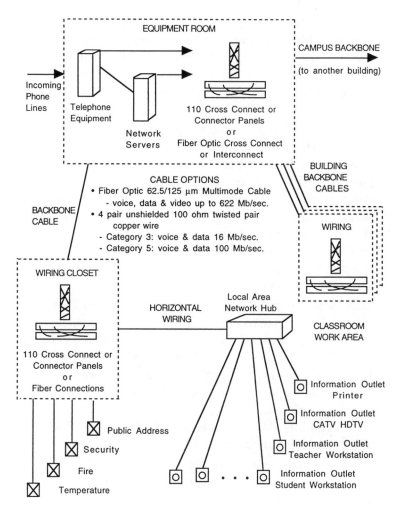

Figure F.1. Structured Communications Cabling System

campus backbone; it has high bandwidth and also provides electrical isolation between the buildings.

• Backbone: backbone wiring (also termed *riser*) is the link between the equipment room and the wiring closets. It is normally installed in a star topology: Cables, radiating from the equipment room, are run to each wiring closet. In some instances, there can be another secondary level of wiring closets. Although risers are used in multistory buildings, they are also necessary in single-floor, spread-out buildings. Because multimedia applications must be anticipated in schools, fiber-optic cable is the medium of choice for backbones.

- Horizontal cabling: provides the link between the wiring closet and the information outlets where the user equipment is attached. These cables are classified as *plenum* or *nonplenum*. Plenum cable can be installed in a plenum—the space above the suspended ceiling used to return air to the heating and cooling system. Plenum cable burns with a low flame, low smoke, and no toxic gases. At present, category 5 unshielded twisted-pair wiring is the medium of choice for horizontal wiring, but this may shift to fiber optic as the economics change.

- Local area network (LAN) hub: Although not strictly a structured cabling system component, the LAN hub is the switching point for data traffic on a classroom local area network. As such, traffic between devices on the LAN is isolated to the LAN, reducing the backbone traffic. Information destined for other places is routed by the hub to its destination via the backbone. Depending on the number of connected devices and the data traffic, a single LAN hub could support a single or several classrooms.

- Work area subsystem: consists of all the cords, adapters, outlets, and transmission electronics to connect user equipment to the network.

- Administration subsystem: ties all the other components together. It consists of patch cords, jumper wires, and circuit identifiers.

Communications and Wiring Standards

The ability of these components to function together now and in the future directly depends on their conformance to accepted standards and specifications. Equipment failing to meet or exceed these standards is an invitation to problems either now or later.

National and industry technical standards are the basis for structured premises wiring. Those persons responsible for specifying, procuring, installing, or administering communications wiring should be intimately familiar with at least the standards listed below. Appendix F, Telecommunications System Construction Specifications, is based on these and related standards. In addition to the technical standards, some companies comply with the ISO 9000 standards addressing company quality processes. ISO 9000 certification is well established in Europe and gaining momentum in the United States, with many leading companies already certified. In the United States, at present, lack of certification should not disqualify a vendor, but qualification should certainly weigh in favor of a company. The following are standards governing communication wiring:

- EIA/TIA (Electronic Industries Association/Telecommunications Industry Association) 568-A, Commercial Building Telecommunications Wiring Standard (This replaces earlier version, 568, as well as EIA/TIA TSB 36 Additional Cable Specifications for Unshielded Twisted-Pair Cables and EIA/TIA TSB 40 Additional Transmission Specifications for Unshielded Twisted-Pair Connecting Hardware.)

  Backbone cable specifications

  Horizontal cable specifications

  Connecting hardware specifications

  Telecommunications outlet specifications

- National Electric Code

  Article 800 (applies to wire cable)

  Article 770 (applies to conductive and nonconductive fiber-optic cable)

Telecommunications System Construction Specifications

BACKGROUND

G Well-drafted construction specifications are essential for achieving a satisfactory telecommunications system. These generic specifications are included to give school personnel responsible for telecommunications wiring an overview of the main ingredients in a well-specified system. These specifications are not a substitute for the services of a qualified communications wiring engineer. BICSI (Building Industry Consulting Service International) certifies communications wiring specialists called registered communications distribution designers (RCDD). Schools should consider requiring contractors to retain an RCDD who will have final responsibility for the project.

The sentences and paragraphs in this appendix are mostly those published by BICSI in their *Telecommunications Distribution Methods Manual* and are reproduced with permission.[1] Specifications for telecommunications systems will vary due to manufacturer variations, local codes, and customer requirements. The specifications here, therefore, should be taken as a guideline and a checklist.

The size and location of the main equipment room and wiring closets should not be an afterthought. The space allocated to them should have neither water pipes nor transformers within them and should not be located immediately below lavatories, shower rooms, or kitchens; neither should they be located in the basement. The Electrical Industries Association (EIA/TIA 569) recommends the following amount of space be allocated to the equipment room:

Number of Workstations	Work Space (square feet)
1-100	150
101-400	400
401-800	800
801-1,200	1,200

If not otherwise located in a data center, network servers as well as the school's general purpose computers and peripheral equipment should be housed in the main equipment room or in close proximity to it. In either case, additional space must be provided for them. Uninterruptable power systems also may be located in the equipment room.

The placement of wiring closets is determined by the cable length limitations and, equally important, ease of access by network technicians. There should be a wiring closet for each wing or major area of a school, and a closet should not serve more than one floor. The EIA/TIA 569 standard suggests the following amount of space be allocated for wiring closets.

Area Served (based on 100 square feet per workstation)	Closet Work Space (square feet)
5,000 sq ft	10 ft × 7 ft
8,000 sq ft	10 ft × 9 ft
10,000 sq ft	10 ft × 11 ft

If network hubs and power protection equipment are to be located in the wiring closets, then additional space must be provided for them.

The electric power distribution system—cables, power protection equipment, and circuit breaker panels—are best located near the communications patch panels and other equipment. If the power and communications equipment are in the same closet, then power cables must be at least 30 cm (1 ft) and transformers 1.2 m (4 ft) away from communications equipment.

In large main equipment rooms, schools should consider specifying raised floors to facilitate wiring and protect the cables from incidental damage. In addition, equipment rooms as well as closets should always be protected by fire detectors and thermal switches that will cut off power to selected electronic equipment if the temperature rises to some preset threshold.

If it is necessary for a school to specify products by a manufacturer's catalog number, it should be for reference only; there may be more suitable or more cost-effective products than those specified. The following clause then should be included: "Substitute products must be mechanically and electrically interchangeable with the specified products. Samples must be submitted for approval; substitutions made without prior approval are at the contractor's risk."

In addition to the technical standards referenced in this specification, some companies comply with the ISO 9000 standards that address company quality processes. ISO 9000 certification is well established in Europe and gaining momentum in the United States, with many leading companies already certified. In the United States, at present, lack of certification should not disqualify a vendor, but qualification should certainly weigh in favor of those having it.

The following are the most common options for filling in the blanks.

Specifications

Applicable Standards

Unless the local code is more stringent, the following standards will be followed, but the National Electrical Code shall always prevail:

- ANSI/NFPA 70—National Electrical Code
- EIA/TIA 568-A— Commercial Building Telecommunications Wiring Standard (replaces EIA/TIA 568, EIA/TIA TSB 36, and TSB 40)
- EIA/TIA 569— Commercial Building Standard for Telecommunications Pathways and Spaces
- EIA/TIA 606— The Administration Standard for the Telecommunications Infrastructure of Commercial Buildings

Service Entrance

Service entrance specifications have not been included here.

Terminating Space

1. The terminating space for the service entrance shall have a 3/4-inch (20 mm) trade size (20 mm) A/C plywood backboard 8 ft (2.4 m) high.
2. The terminating space shall include a _(A)_ AC power outlet(s) and lighting intensity of _(B)_ .
   - (A) 110 V, 20 ampere
   - (B) 540 lux (50 foot-candles) 1 meter (3 ft) above the floor
3. If the terminating space is not within the equipment room, it shall be secured by a door _____ and installed with a lock.
   - Size: H × W × D—minimum recommended width is 36 inches (90 cm).

Main Communications Room

1. The main equipment room door shall be _____ and installed with a lock.
   - Size H × W × D—the minimum recommended width is 36 inches (90 cm).
2. Backboards constructed of 3/4-inch trade size (20 mm) A/C plywood 8 ft (2.4 m) high shall be rigidly installed and

painted with a nonconductive, fire-retardant overcoat (light in color).

3. Equipment racks shall be secured and grounded.

4. The main equipment room will be configured to accommodate the following ancillary equipment as described in these specifications (list). Unless otherwise specified by the equipment manufacturers, working space of 1 m (3 ft) will be provided in front of all equipment and a similar space provided behind rack-mounted equipment or equipment cabinets.

   - Include copies of manufacturers' installation specifications for all equipment, such as telephone switches, modems, multiplexors, servers, and power conditioners planned for the equipment room. Also specify an amount of additional space for unforeseen additional equipment.

5. The main equipment room will have sufficient power for all ancillary equipment and shall, in addition, include a minimum of two 120-V (A) duplex outlets, each on a separate branch circuit.

   - 20 ampere

6. Light intensity shall be at least _____.

   - 540 lux (50 foot-candles) 1 m (3 ft) above the floor

7. The temperature of the main equipment room shall be kept between ____ degrees.

   - 18°C and 24°C (64°F and 75°F)

8. Humidity in the main equipment room shall be kept between _____ relative humidity.

   - 30% and 55%

9. Ventilation shall accomplish at least one air change per hour.

10. Floors shall be static free, using asphalt or linoleum tile.

11. Emergency lighting shall be provided.

12. The rated distributed floor loading shall be greater than _____.

    - 12 kPa (250 lbf/ft^2)

13. The rated concentrated floor loading shall be greater than
    _____.
    - 4.4 kN (1,000 lbf)

Communications Wiring Closets

1. Wiring closets shall not have door sills or center posts. The door shall be _____ and installed with a lock.
   - Size H × W × D—the minimum recommended width is 36 inches (90 cm).
2. Two walls of the closet shall be lined with rigidly installed, wall-to-wall framing of trade size 3/4-inch (20 mm) A/C plywood 8 ft (2.4 m) high. They shall be painted with a nonconductive, fire-retarding overcoat (light in color).
3. Sleeves or dam walls around the floor slots shall extend _____.
   - Use a value between 2.5 mm (1 in.) and 100 mm (4 in.) above the floor.
4. All sleeves shall be fire stopped.
5. Conduit(s) and cable tray(s) located in the ceiling shall protrude _____ into the closet.
   - Use a value between 2.5 cm (1 in.) and 100 mm (4 in.)
6. Equipment racks shall be secured and grounded.
7. The wiring closet will be configured to accommodate the following ancillary equipment as described in these specifications _(list)_ . Unless otherwise specified by the equipment manufacturers, working space of 1 m (3 ft) will be provided in front of all equipment and a similar space provided behind rack-mounted equipment or equipment cabinets.
   - Include copies of manufacturers' installation specifications for all equipment, including telephone switches, modems, multiplexors, and power conditioners, planned in the equipment room. Also specify an amount of additional space for unforeseen additional equipment.

8. The wiring closet will have sufficient power for all ancillary equipment and shall, in addition, include a minimum of two 120-V (A) duplex outlets on separate branch circuits and at least (B) 120-V AC convenience outlet.
   - (A) 120-V AC
   - (B) two
9. Lighting in the closet shall be at least _____.
   - 540 lux (50 foot-candles) 1 m (3 ft) above the floor
10. The temperature of the closet shall be kept between ____ degrees.
    - 10°C and 35°C (59°F and 95°F)
11. Humidity in the closet shall be kept between _____ relative humidity.
    - 30% and 55%
12. Ventilation shall accomplish at least one air change per hour.
13. Floors shall be static free, using asphalt or linoleum tile.
14. The rated distributed floor loading shall be greater than _____.
    - 2.4 kPA (50 lbf/ft^2)

Backbone Cable

1. Each (A) backbone cable shall be no longer than (B) .

A	B
1. 62.5/125 multimode fiber	1. 2,000 m (6,600 ft)
2. 100 ohm unshielded twisted pair	2. 800 m (2,600 ft)
3. 150 ohm unshielded twisted pair	3. 700 m (2,300 ft)
4. 50 ohm unshielded twisted pair	4. 500 m (1,600 ft)
5. 75 ohm unshielded twisted pair	5. 500 m (1,600 ft)
6. Single-mode fiber	6. 3,000 m (9,800 ft)

Note: Selections from columns A and B shall have matching numbers (e.g., A2 must be paired with B2).

2. Cable support shall be provided by _____
   - Conduits
   - Cable trays
   - Strand
   - Clamping cables to plywood backboard in each closet

Grounding, Bonding, and Electrical Protection

1. The grounding system shall not rely on plumbing systems.
2. Bonding connectors shall be routed with a minimum number of bends. The bends placed in the conductor should be sweeping.
3. All bonding connections shall be made with listed bolts, crimp pressure connectors, clamps, or lugs. Exothermic welding may be used.
4. Multiple bus bars placed in a building shall be directly bonded with #6 AWG copper conductor.
5. Backbone cabling shall be bonded at each sheath opening.

Horizontal Distribution Wiring

A variety of pathways for the horizontal distribution are available. These distribution pathways and their construction specifications are described in Chapter 4, "Horizontal Cabling Systems" in the *Telecommunications Distributions Methods Manual* available from BICSI.

ADA Guidelines

All guidelines of the American Disabilities Act (ADA) shall be incorporated into the construction specifications for the horizontal wiring systems.

Pathways

To avoid electromagnetic interference (EMI), all pathways shall provide clearances of at least _____.

- 1.2 m (4 ft) from large motors and transformers
- 30 cm (1 ft) from conduit and cables used for electric power
- 12 cm (5 in.) from fluorescent lighting

Cabling

Note: The following cabling construction specifications are recommended. However, other cabling approaches not addressed here may be appropriate in certain situations.

1. The distance between the termination in the communications closet and the information outlet shall be _____ or less.
   - 90 m (295 ft)
2. The length of patch cords and interconnect jumpers in the telecommunications closet shall be _____ or less.
   - 6 m (20 ft)
3. No more than _____ horizontal cables from the telecommunications closet to an outlet shall be used in a star topology.
   - Two
4. Horizontal cabling shall not have more than _____ transition point between different forms of the same cable type (i.e., from round cable to flat undercarpet cable).
   - One
5. Horizontal cable shall be grounded in compliance with the National Electrical Code (ANSI/NFPA 70) requirements and practices, except where superseded by other authorities or codes. In addition to horizontal cables, these grounding requirements apply to all horizontal-distribution wiring.
   - Cross-connect frames
   - Patch panel racks
   - Active telecommunications equipment
   - Test apparatus used for maintenance and testing
6. Mount outlets securely at work area locations.

7. Work area outlets shall be located so the cable required to reach work area equipment will be no longer than 3 m (10 ft).

8. Electrical components (e.g., impedance matching devices) at the outlets shall be outside the face plate via a standard plug connection.

9. All connectors providing electrical connections between 100 ohm UTP cables shall meet the requirements of ANSI/TIA/EIA-568-A.

10. All connectors providing electrical connections between 150 ohm STP cables shall meet the requirements of ANSI/TIA/EIA-568-A.

11. Installation and connection of horizontal fiber-optic cabling shall conform to ANSI/TIA/EIA-568-A.

12. 100 ohm horizontal cable shall conform to EIA/TIA/EIA-568-A category 3, 4, or 5.

13. Extended performance STP cable and connectors shall conform to UL subjects 444 and 13 (STP) (Ref. 7.19).

Sound Systems

1. Ceiling speakers shall be placed in a staggered pattern with the distance between speakers, placed in a row, being approximately _____ the ceiling height.
   - Twice

2. Wall-mounted speakers shall be mounted at least _____ above the floor.
   - 2 meters (6.5 ft)

3. Where the depth of the area to be covered does not exceed _____, the speakers can be mounted on the same wall. If the depth of the coverage is over _____ , the speakers shall be mounted on opposite walls in a strategic configuration.
   - 9 m (30 ft)

4. For cable lengths _(A)_ , use No. 18 wire or larger. For cable lengths greater than _(B)_ , use No. 16 wire or larger.
   - (A) 15 m to 30 m (50 ft to 100 ft)
   - (B) 31 m (101 ft)

Acceptance Testing

The contractor will provide the school with a recommended acceptance test procedure that will validate the school's requirements as contained in the contract. The contractor will avail the school of the opportunity to be present at all tests.

Warranty

The contractor will provide a written _____-year material and labor warranty for all passive components. The warranty will include claim procedures and the means of dispute resolution.

- 15

Documentation

1. Consistent with EIA/TIA 606 Administration Standards for the Telecommunications Infrastructure of Commercial Buildings, the contractor will clearly mark and label all pathways, cables (both ends), spaces, grounding, termination hardware, and termination positions.
2. Upon contract completion, the contractor will provide the school with as-built drawings and records showing all pathways, cables (both ends), spaces, grounding, termination hardware, and termination positions. A record of the model number and serial number of all installed equipment also will be provided.
3. Upon contract completion the contractor will provide the school with a copy of all equipment and cable test results.
4. The contractor may provide documentation in an electronic media if the format is acceptable to the school.

Training

The contractor will provide training to _____ school personnel.
- At least two

The training will include the following topics (describe) .

- Review of all documentation and test results
- Walk-through of all locations
- Troubleshooting and maintenance procedures

Note

1. BICSI, 10500 University Center Drive, Suite 100, Tampa, FL 33612-6415.

Secret Versus Public Key Cryptography

The nature of most types of electronic communications is inherently insecure. Telephone wires are easily tapped, and radio transmissions can be monitored by any person with an antenna. If there is a need for private electronics communications, then cryptography is the means. Depending on the method and the size of the key, messages, for all practical purposes, can be indecipherable. There are two basic cryptographic methods: secret key and public key.

The idea of a secret key scheme is that both parties share a single key that they use both to encrypt and decrypt the messages they exchange. Whenever the key is changed, a secure (nonelectronic) means must be found to deliver the new key to all the correspondents. If the key is compromised, security is lost.

A public key system uses a set of two mated keys. Each person has two keys; one of them is a public key, and the other is a private key. The public key, which is available to anybody, is used by a message sender to encrypt the message. The receiver's unique private key is used by the receiver to decrypt the message. Because the private key is not shared, there is no need for a separate, secure means to distribute keys. Also, each person has the capa-

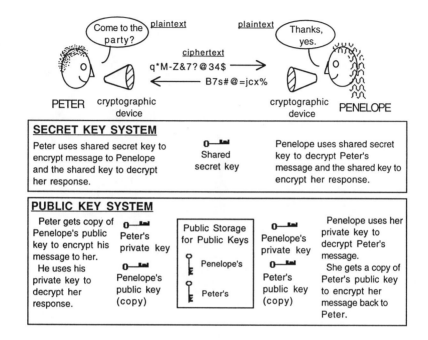

Figure H.1. Public Key Versus Private Key Cryptography

bility to change his or her key set at will and to do so without the knowledge or cooperation of others.

The public key system also provides an electronic signature capability. The sender encrypts his or her signature with the private key, and the receiver decrypts it with the sender's public key—this verifies the sender's identity.

References

Allen, G. W., & Segall, D. (1974, January 27-February 1). *Monitoring of computer installations for power line disturbances.* Paper presented at the meeting of the IEEE Power Engineering Society, New York.

American Academy of Ophthalmology. (1992, February 15). *Information about eye care— Video display terminals (VDTs) and the eye.* San Francisco: Author.

American National Standards Institute. (1990). *Commercial building standard for telecommunications pathways and spaces ANSI/EIA/TIA Standard 569.* New York: Author.

Apple Computer. (1991). *Apple classrooms of tomorrow: Philosophy and structure.* Cupertino, CA: Author.

Armstrong, T. (1994). *Multiple intelligences in the classroom.* Alexandria, VA: Association for Supervision and Curriculum Development.

Artificial intelligence. (1994, March). *Communications of the ACM, 37*(3).

Bardelli, L., Cavara, V., & Bietti, G. B. (1989). Epidemiologic survey of ocular disorders among VDT operators: An Italian multicentric research on 31,570 subjects. *Bolletino di Oculistica, 68*(Suppl. 7), 3-123.

Building Industry Consulting Service International (BICSI). (1996). *Telecommunications distribution methods manual.* Tampa, FL: Author.

Bluestein, W. M., Colony, G. F., & Chowdhury, S. (1994, October). *Home PCs: The golden age—Executive summary.* Cambridge, MA: Forrester Research.

Brown, S. (1993). *Preventing computer injury: The handbook.* New York: Ergonomic.

Carolyn Burst v. Apple Computer, Inc. (CA. 950200, 1995).

The Center for Governmental Responsibility, College of Law, University of Florida. (Ed.). (1994). *Legal issues for the design and development of a technology-supported system of education: 1993-1994 legal memoranda.* Tallahassee: Florida State University (distributor), Center for Educational Technology.

Chaffin, D. B. (1991). *Occupational biomechanics.* New York: Wiley-Interscience.

Computer waves. (1990, September 10). *U.S. News & World Report,* pp. 83-86.

Copyright Act, 17 U.S.C. §106.

Dolan, C. (1994, June 27). Off course. *Wall Street Journal,* p. R16.

End-user training and learning. (1995, July). *Communications of the ACM, 38*(7).

Flanders, B. (1994, October). A delicate balance. *School Library Journal,* pp. 32-35.

Frisch, A. (1994, February). Fencebuilding 104. *RS/Magazine, 3*(2), 20.

Gardner, H. (1993). *Frames of mind: The theory of multiple intelligences.* New York: Basic Books.

Georgia Department of Education—Division of Instructional Technology. (1994, March). *Modernizing learning environments with educational technology.* Atlanta: Author.

Goldstein, M., & Speranza, P. D. (1982, October). *The quality of U.S. commercial ac power.* Paper presented at the Fourth International Telecommunications Energy Conference (IN-TELEC), Washington, DC.

Graham Oil v. Arco Products Co., 43 F3d 1244 (9th Cir. 1994).

Hausman, E. (1994, November 13). Network failure "downtime" costs on the rise. *Computer Reseller News,* p. 6.

The Institute of Electrical and Electronics Engineers (IEEE). (1987). *IEEE recommended practice for emergency power and standby power systems.* New York: Author.

The Institute of Electrical and Electronics Engineers (IEEE). (1992). *IEEE recommended practice for powering and grounding sensitive electronic equipment.* New York: Author.

International Labour Organization. (1994). *Visual display units: Radiation protection guidance* (Occupational Safety and Health series No. 70). Geneva, Switzerland: Author.

Machiavelli, N. (1952). *The prince* (E. P. R. Vincent, Trans.). New York: New American Library of World Literature. (Original publication 1513)

Milam, J. E. (1992). *Underfloor air distribution HVAC system analysis.* Marietta, GA: Environmental Design International.

Moore, S. D. (1994, June 27). Making it friendly. *Wall Street Journal,* p. R15.

Mow, S. L., & Freweouf, B. C. (1994). *Report on a project to integrate technology into required preservice teacher education courses at nine Westchester colleges and universities.* White Plains, NY: The Westchester Education Coalition.

National Education Association. (1994). *Resolutions, legislative program, and new business 1994-95.* Washington, DC: Author.

Neumann, P. G. (1994, March). Technology, laws, and society. *Communications of the ACM, 37*(3), 138.

9to5, National Association of Working Women. (n.d.-a). *An introduction to office health and safety.* Cleveland, OH: Author.

9to5, National Association of Working Women. (n.d.-b). *Computer health and safety.* Cleveland, OH: Author.

9to5, National Association of Working Women. (n.d.-c). *VDTs, pregnancy, and radiation.* Cleveland, OH: Author.

Piller, C. (1992, September). Separate realities. *Macworld, 9*(9), 8-21.

Playboy Enterprises v. Frena, 839 F.Supp. 1552 (M.D.Fla. 1993).

Prudential Insurance Co. of America v. Lai, 42 F 3d 1299 (9th Cir. 1994).

Rea, M. S. (1991, October). Solving the problem of VDT reflections. *Progressive Architecture,* pp. 35-40.

Reich, R. (1991). *The work of nations.* New York: Knopf.

Richards, B. (1994, July 14). Cancer link to electromagnetic fields recognized in Washington state ruling. *Wall Street Journal,* p. B3.

Rockart, J. F., & Bullen, C. V. (1986). *The rise of managerial computing.* Homewood, IL: Dow Jones-Irwin.

Rose, S. J. (1994). *On shaky ground: Rising fears about incomes and earnings* (Research Report No. 94-02). Washington, DC: National Commission for Employment Policy.

Sandberg, J. (1994, August 18). Losses linked to lax security of computers. *Wall Street Journal,* p. B4.

Sellers, D. (1994). *Zap! How your computer can hurt you—and what you can do about it.* Berkeley, CA: Peachpit Press.

Smith, H. (1995). *Rethinking America.* New York: Random House.

Software Publishers Association. (1994). *The K-12 guide to legal software use.* Washington, DC: Author.

Sony Corporation of America v. Universal City Studios, Inc., 464 US 417,435 (1983).

Steelcase, Inc. (1991a). *Steelcase office environment index summary report—United States.* Grand Rapids, MI: Author.

Steelcase, Inc. (1991b). *Worldwide office environment index facility management white paper.* Grand Rapids, MI: Author.

Strassmann, P. A. (1985). *Information payoff.* New York: Macmillan.

Strassmann, P. A. (1995). *The politics of information management—Policy guidelines.* New Canaan, CT: The Information Economics Press.

Stratton Oakmont, Inc. and Daniel Poruse v. Prodigy Services Co. (NY. 31063/94, 1995).

Stuebing, S., Giddings, J., & Cousineau L. K. (1992). *Technology-rich learning environments in elementary and secondary schools: An interactive study of physical settings and educational change.* Cupertino, CA: Apple Computer, Apple Classrooms of Tomorrow.

Stuebing, S., Knox, L., Petrakaki, M., & Giddings, J. (1991). *Vision for the future learning environment.* Newark: New Jersey Institute of Technology, Giddings School of Architecture.

Stuebing, S., Martin, E., Wolfshorndl, A., & Cousineau, L. (1992). *School design notebook.* Newark: New Jersey Institute of Technology.

Telecommunications Industry Association. (1994, March). *Fiber vs. copper in high data rate LAN applications.* Arlington, VA: Author.

Times Mirror Center for the People & the Press. (1994). *The role of technology in American life.* Washington, DC: Times Mirror Company.

U.S. Department of Education. (1994). *The sixteenth annual report to Congress on the implementation of the Individuals With Disabilities Education Act.* Washington, DC: Government Printing Office.

U.S. Department of Education, National Center for Education Statistics. (1993). *Dropout rates in the United States: 1992* (NCES Publication No. NCES 93-464). Washington, DC: Government Printing Office.

U.S. General Accounting Office. (1995). *Information superhighway—An overview of technology challenges—GAO/AIMD-95-23.* Washington, DC: Author.

Vijayan, J. (1995, February 13). LAN servers flourish; support stays in flux. *Computerworld, 29*(7), 39, 45.

Webster's new Riverside desk quotations. (1992). New York: Houghton Mifflin.

Whalen, R. (1994, June 24). *Public high school graduates, 1991-92, compared with 9th grade enrollment in fall 1988 by state* (Unpublished report). Washington, DC: Department of Education, National Center for Education Statistics.

Yankelovich Partners. (1995). *Report of Time/CNN poll conducted January 25-26.* Claremont, CA: Author.

Yarn, D. H. (1992). *Alternative dispute resolution—Practice and procedure in Georgia.* Norcross, GA: Harrison Company.

Yates, J. C., & Arne, P. H. (1994). Technology law. *Atlanta Computer Currents, 6*(1), 42.

Yoder, S. K. (1994, November 14). When things go wrong. *Wall Street Journal,* p. R16.

Index

CORWIN
PRESS

The Corwin Press logo—a raven striding across an open book—represents the happy union of courage and learning. We are a professional-level publisher of books and journals for K-12 educators, and we are committed to creating and providing resources that embody these qualities. Corwin's motto is "Success for All Learners."